DISCOVER YOUR REPRESSED POWERS

TRY ASTRAL PROJECTION

HONE YOUR INTUITION

CHANNEL SPIRITS

LOOK INTO THE FUTURE

PSYCHIC HEALING

HOW TO BE A
PSYCHIC

MICHAEL R. HATHAWAY

ADAMS MEDIA

NEW YORK   LONDON   TORONTO   SYDNEY   NEW DELHI

Adams Media
An Imprint of Simon & Schuster, Inc.
57 Littlefield Street
Avon, Massachusetts 02322

Copyright © 2017 by Simon & Schuster, Inc.

All rights reserved, including the right to reproduce this book or portions thereof in any form whatsoever. For information address Adams Media Subsidiary Rights Department, 1230 Avenue of the Americas, New York, NY 10020.

First Adams Media trade paperback edition DEC 2016

ADAMS MEDIA and colophon are trademarks of Simon and Schuster.

For information about special discounts for bulk purchases, please contact Simon & Schuster Special Sales at 1-866-506-1949 or business@ simonandschuster.com.

The Simon & Schuster Speakers Bureau can bring authors to your live event. For more information or to book an event contact the Simon & Schuster Speakers Bureau at 1-866-248-3049 or visit our website at www.simonspeakers.com.

Contains material adapted from *The Everything® Psychic Book, 2nd Edition* by Michael R. Hathaway, DCH, copyright © 2011 by Simon & Schuster, Inc., ISBN 13: 978-1-4405-2702-9.

Interior images © Daria Solomennikova/123RF

Manufactured in the United States of America

10 9 8 7 6 5 4

Library of Congress Cataloging-in-Publication Data has been applied for.

ISBN 978-1-5072-0061-2
ISBN 978-1-5072-0062-9 (ebook)

Many of the designations used by manufacturers and sellers to distinguish their products are claimed as trademarks. Where those designations appear in this book and Simon & Schuster, Inc., was aware of a trademark claim, the designations have been printed with initial capital letters.

CONTENTS

INTRODUCTION

You may think psychic powers are rare, but the truth is that *everyone* possesses psychic abilities. You just need the right tools to uncover and develop them. *How to Be a Psychic* will show you how to control and help you recognize your own unique psychic talent. You'll find everything from connecting to your third eye and reading auras to communicating with the spirit world and practicing psychic healing. Above all, you'll get the tools you need to interpret your own psychic power as a way of delving deep into your inner being.

You were born with at least one special psychic gift. And whether your talent lies in clairvoyance, clairaudience, psychic healing, spirit communication, astral projection, mediumship, or animal communication—this comprehensive guide will help you explore and utilize it.

As you become more familiar with your psychic ability, you will be able to gain insights into yourself and your future. You will learn to enter a state of focus, find your balance, and connect to the powers you have within yourself. You will be able to meet your spirit guides, work with energies, and even receive information through your dreams. Your psychic gift is waiting to be discovered and set into positive use.

Now let's begin a journey through the mysterious and fascinating world of psychic powers.

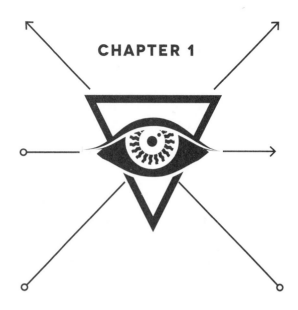

CHAPTER 1

PSYCHIC ABILITIES 101

Did you know that you are psychic? You are, even though you may not think so. Many people do not understand this special natural ability. It is often unwelcome and misunderstood, not only by psychics themselves but by family, friends, and strangers alike. This chapter will provide you with an introduction into the psychic world and what it means to be psychic. You will learn about the levels of consciousness, psychic intuition, and how to enter a state of focus. You'll also learn how to connect to your third eye, a location in the body through which many psychics receive their information.

DISCOVERING WHAT IS INSIDE YOU

Everyone is psychic. You were born with at least one special gift already imprinted in your soul. Everything that you have experienced so far in this lifetime has helped develop your ability. Your psychic ability, like any other talent or characteristic, is a product of your physical self, your environment, your relationships, and your inherited genetics. Remember that you are the keeper of your own ability. It is there waiting to be set into positive use. No matter what you read or others tell you, it is your soul that knows the answers. The goal here is for you to identify and become comfortable with your own special psychic abilities.

The word "psychic" comes from the Greek word for "psyche," also meaning "spirit" or "soul." In Greek mythology, Psyche, a girl who loved one of the gods and suffered through many trials because of it, personifies the soul. Through her suffering, she became a great soul (or soulful).

Unfortunately, the idea of being psychic often conjures up the image of gypsy fortunetellers or pay-per-minute phone psychics. Some who pretend to be psychic only want to fleece you out of your hard-earned money with their "mystical insights." They are masters at tricking their clients into giving them information they can use as if it came from the realm of the psychic. You might also find books that discuss how to develop and use your hidden psychic power to help you control the world around you. Manifesting your destiny, enjoying perfect health, and finding wealth and prosperity are popular subjects, thanks to books such as *The Secret*. As a result, many people try to misuse their gifts for self-gain rather than to benefit the Universe and help others along the pathways of life.

Because it is different for every person, it is impossible to explain exactly what the psychic process is like. No one else has a mind that is identical to yours. Many psychic courses designed to enhance intuitive abilities are presented in a model that the instructor uses. However if you, the participant, are not of a similar mind, your initial enthusiasm can easily turn to frustration.

Some people see life as a battlefield. They constantly face one crisis after another. They find themselves drained of any creative energy that could help them move forward. They do not know how to step back and find a different view of a situation. They do not understand that their own failure to recognize their intuitive guidance system, which is in place and waiting to be set in motion, is part of their dilemma.

Try to think of it like this: Each soul has a map to follow during its lifetime. The map should be used as a guide to learning life lessons and resolving old karma. Whether you choose to follow this map or not is your individual choice—your free will. It is your free will to choose to become in tune with your psychic ability.

YOUR PSYCHIC INTUITION

You exist almost simultaneously in three different minds.

* The **conscious mind** is your thinking mind and is aware of the events taking place around you.

* Your **unconscious mind** is the place where all of your memories are stored. It is constantly sending images up to your conscious mind.

* Your unconscious mind connects you to your third mind, **the Universal Mind** that is the source of all knowledge in the Universe, including the present, the past, and the future.

There are three types of psychic intuition: deductive, random, and goal-focused. Deductive intuition comes from the unconscious mind, random intuition comes from the Universal Mind, and goal-focused intuition works through all three minds. Your mental makeup determines the type of intuition that is yours. Each person has a unique form of intuition that may be a blend of any of the three types.

Your mind receives external stimuli through five different senses: sight, sound, touch, taste, and smell. You remember past experiences internally through these same five senses. Each person, however, processes these memories in different ways.

Deductive Psychic Intuition

Deductive psychic images come from your unconscious mind's ability to take in external sensory stimuli. That's not as complicated as it sounds. Your five sensory receivers—eyes, ears, mouth, skin, and nose—are constantly bombarded with stimuli in the form of external pictures, sounds, tastes, tactile sensations, temperature changes, and smells. You also experience external emotions or energies unrecognized by your conscious mind. You take in a lot of information that you are not consciously aware of because it is absorbed by the unconscious mind, where it is stored.

When your conscious mind has a question that it cannot answer, this question will also go to the unconscious mind, which will mull over the problem and rely on its stored data to come up with a response. In the meantime, your conscious mind usually goes on to another subject and forgets what it was looking for. But your unconscious mind stays hard at work. All of a sudden, out of nowhere, a psychic insight appears. Your unconscious mind has come to a logical psychic solution to your problem, one that your conscious mind hadn't thought of.

Random Psychic Intuition

Random psychic intuition is different from deductive psychic intuition in several ways. It comes from your Universal Mind and may be totally unrelated to anything known or connected consciously or unconsciously to the psychic image. It could be about something that has taken, is taking, or will take place anywhere in the world. In other words, random psychic intuition can take place in any of the three phases of time—past, present, or future.

A random psychic experience often comes at a time when it is unexpected or even unwanted. It can be very powerful and leave you dazed and confused. This disorientation may last only a few moments, but its effects are powerful enough to last a lifetime. The experience itself may continue to live on in your mind long after the image first appears.

Not all random psychic experiences are negative. It is possible that you might have a pleasant premonition; then later, you might realize that what you saw as nothing more than a happy daydream has become a reality. It may be that you suddenly get a set of numbers in your head that leads to a big sweepstake jackpot win. Or a song may begin to play in your head that you haven't heard in years, a song that later you may unexpectedly hear on the radio or television.

Random psychic intuition happens when you are in a light trance state. It occurs when your conscious or critical mind is open to the images that are sent up from your unconscious and your Universal Mind. A random psychic trance can be triggered by external or internal stimuli. Once the intuitive trance process begins, it is hard to disengage from it until it has run its course.

Goal-Focused Psychic Intuition

Goal-focused psychic intuition is a combination of deductive and random intuition. Using this method, you can make a conscious effort to gain certain insights through psychic intuition. You can attempt to use your intuitive ability for a specific goal. Focused psychic intuition is the kind that is normally employed by professional psychics and others who already understand and use their intuitive abilities on a consistent basis.

When you ask a fortuneteller to give you an answer about a specific problem in your life, the psychic will connect to her intuitive source and focus on the requested information. Then she waits for her mind to download the information requested.

Professional psychics who work with the police will often familiarize themselves with some of the facts of the case they are working on. Examining a piece of evidence or a photograph from a crime scene could provide intuitive information, and an actual visit to a specific location may also lead to new clues. Some of the information may be drawn from deductive intuition, and some may be generated at random, but all clues gathered are related to the specific goal of the psychic trance.

ENTERING A STATE OF FOCUS

When your conscious mind's ability to think clearly is interrupted, you enter an altered state of focus. All people, whether they know it or not, go in and out of this state many times a day. When there, your critical reasoning is pushed aside. The power of suggestion, whether it's by your unconscious mind or by someone else, takes control of your thought process.

You can be guided or induced into a trance in several different ways. The trigger can come either through external stimuli—if, for instance, you were to enter a specific location—or through internal stimuli, such as thoughts or feelings. Trances can be positive or negative, and they can continue to influence you long after your initial experience. You can remain in a trance state for a few minutes or for days. The state will continue until something interrupts it. Once you recognize the trance state, you have the choice of remaining in it or not.

An altered state of consciousness occurs when a person is not necessarily aware of what he or she is experiencing. The conscious mind is not involved in making critical decisions. The person in a deep state may have no knowledge of external events.

Moving Through Time

Your mind moves through three different phases of time: the past, the present, and the future. Everything that you have experienced in your lifetime—your past—is deposited in the memory bank of your unconscious mind. Sometimes the information is held there for years before it suddenly comes back up to the surface of your conscious mind. When you experience these memories again, you have actually focused on a memory-induced altered state of consciousness. The stronger the memory, the stronger the focus.

It is also possible to focus on a future experience in the same way that you focus on a past experience. Some people have vivid images of events that are yet to happen. These images can come to the surface of the unconscious mind without warning when you are in a relaxed mind or even while you are dreaming.

Your mind also experiences the present. In this time phase, it can distort speed and distance. Sometimes a minute seems like an hour, and sometimes an hour seems like a minute. In athletics, being in the present is called "being in the zone."

Have you ever driven down the highway and become so absorbed in thought that you actually went right by your destination? You were in an altered state of focus when this occurred. Even though you were not totally aware of your location, you were still driving your vehicle safely. This phenomenon is called highway hypnosis.

It is easy to get caught up in such an altered state of focus that you are unaware of what time phase you are in. This can be very confusing when it happens without warning. As you learn to balance the three phases of your mind and be aware of the past, the future, and the present altered states, it will be easier to understand how your mind focuses.

Psychic Altered States of Focus

Psychic altered states of focus occur when your conscious mind is flooded with information that cannot be deduced by critical reasoning. Usually, this information comes from the unconscious and/ or the Universal Mind, and it often comes at a time when you are least expecting it. Knowing what is going on within yourself is the key to being in tune with these altered states.

Everyone enters into one or more kinds of psychic altered states. Some have a great deal of meaning, while others seem to be there just to verify that you are capable of experiencing something unexplainable. Perhaps you have experienced knowing when the telephone was going to ring or thought of a song just before it played on the radio.

FINDING YOUR BALANCE

Here is a suggestion to help you find an inner balance of mind. Create a place in your mind where you can escape for a few moments, and learn to relax there. For some of you, this may seem impossible. If relaxing for you at this time is difficult, don't worry. As you progress through the book, you will learn how to find your balance.

You may already be familiar with the term "centering yourself." Many situations in your life can keep you from being centered. You may be kept off balance by the people around you, the environment, or by psychic information when it pours through the unconscious mind. It is easy to be overwhelmed by all the stimuli, both external and internal. To help deal with life's uncertainties, you need to learn how to center yourself.

Exercise: Connect with Your Third Eye

Your third eye, a spot of mental focus, is located between and above your two eyes in the center of your forehead. It is the point of connection to your sixth chakra, which is often associated with your pituitary gland (a small gland the size of a pea located at the base of your brain). All three of your eyes together form the points of a triangle, a symbol that is found throughout ancient history, especially in the society of the pyramid builders. Perhaps they were aware of some lost ancient secret that helped them connect to the eye of the soul.

Focus Upward

An easy way to center yourself is to make a connection with your third eye. Those of you with a religious background may connect with your third eye when you pray. You can also do it through meditation. Another approach of connecting with your third eye is by doing the following exercise.

If for some reason you are uncomfortable about connecting to your third eye, don't feel that you have to try. All the exercises in this book are designed for you to have a positive experience. If at any time you are not comfortable, you may simply stop and return to a more positive feeling.

For a moment, look upward with your two physical eyes as if you were trying to see your third eye. If for some reason this is impossible or hard for you to do, that's okay; it is not actually necessary to move or see through your two eyes to experience this. You may keep your two eyes open or closed while you peek up under your eyelids. Some of you may want to squint slightly and feel your third eye.

When you try this, you may feel a slight pressure in your third eye. It may feel like it is swelling or even vibrating. You may have a feeling of warmth or coolness, or you may perceive a certain color. Whatever you experience is okay—it's also possible that you won't feel anything at all.

Each person will connect to her third eye in a way that is natural and correct for her. Remember, there is no one else exactly like you. No one else will have the experience that you have when you communicate through your third eye.

Breathe

Now let's add something else to help you center yourself when you connect to your third eye. You may want to take a moment and find a comfortable place to sit or lie down. If any of your clothing is tight, you may want to loosen it a little. It is not absolutely necessary, but it may help you to become a little more centered. When you have done this, you may allow yourself to feel a connection with your third eye.

For a moment, allow yourself to get comfortable with the sensations you are experiencing as you make this connection. When you're ready, take a deep breath at a level that feels right for you. It may not be easy for you to inhale deeply, and that's okay. What is important is for you to breathe at a pace that helps you strengthen the connection with your third eye.

Continue to breathe slowly for a few minutes. It doesn't matter whether you keep your eyes open or closed—whatever way feels right for you is correct. Your mind may just drift away. It may also be very active, with lots of thoughts suddenly popping up, or it may focus on one thing.

Some people get frustrated trying to learn to meditate. They are instructed to quiet their mind, but they find it impossible to do. If your mind is that way, don't worry about it; just breathe and focus on your third eye.

After you have experienced the results of this exercise for a length of time that is comfortable for you, you may take a deep breath. As you exhale, release the connection with your third eye and come back to the surface of your mind refreshed and relaxed. The more you practice this, the easier it will be to make a positive connection. Focusing on your third eye is a great way to begin connecting to your psychic mind.

EDGAR CAYCE, FATHER OF THE NEW AGE

The largest impact on the advancement of psychic knowledge was made by a man named Edgar Cayce (1877–1945), who is now considered to be the founder of the New Age movement. Cayce spent much of his life trying to understand what he did while he was in a trance. While in trance, he spoke about unknown civilizations in which the soul hadn't yet developed a physical body and was free to travel about without the restriction of gravity and to communicate through thought.

Cayce indicated in his readings that souls were originally thought-forms that were not destined to inhabit the earth; rather they were early observers of life here that became so intrigued with its development that they chose to enter these life forms and then became trapped. When a soul leaves its physical body at death, it still exists on a nonphysical plane. Some people have unconscious memories of what it was like to exist in pure thought form. You may have soul memories of those early times that can help in your psychic development.

An Unlikely Psychic

Cayce was an unlikely candidate for reaching the pinnacle of acclaim that he still enjoys today, more than a half-century since his death. He began life in rural Kentucky's tobacco country. He was close to his grandfather, Thomas Jefferson Cayce, who was said to have special psychic abilities.

Tragedy struck one day when young Cayce witnessed the death of his grandfather in an accident with a horse. After the incident, young Edgar would visit his grandfather's spirit in one of the barns. Cayce's grandmother and mother encouraged him to continue these visits and to tell them about his experiences.

Many calamities befell young Edgar. When he was three, he fell against a fence post and punctured his skull on a nail, possibly deep enough to reach his brain. His father poured turpentine in the wound, and Cayce recovered in a short period of time. At fifteen, he was hit on the spine by a ball and began to act strangely. After his father sent him to bed, he entered a hypnotic trance, telling his father what to do to cure him. His father followed the directions, and Cayce awoke the next morning his normal self.

When he was in his early twenties, he lost his voice. A traveling stage hypnotist temporarily helped him, and he learned to enter a self-hypnotic trance aided by a local man named Al Layne, who had taken a mail-order course on the subject. While in this altered state, Cayce was able to give himself the cure for his voice blockage. His throat turned bright red, he coughed up some blood, and his voice returned. Over the next year, Cayce's voice would need further treatment on a monthly basis, and Layne, intrigued by Cayce's diagnostic abilities, experimented with his subject, hoping to uncover answers to his talent.

Edgar Cayce and Extrasensory Perception

In 1931, Cayce and his supporters formed the Association for Research and Enlightenment for the purpose of studying, researching, and disseminating information about extrasensory perception, or ESP, as well as dreams, holistic health, and life after death. The center was located in Virginia Beach, where it remains today.

Cayce was able to use his psychic abilities in four different areas: precognition, retrocognition, clairvoyance, and telepathy. He had the ability to see into the future and give predictions of events to come. He could look into a person's past to find the origins of an existing health condition. He had the physical ability to see through objects and could see the inside of the human body. He was also able to enter another mind and know what the person was thinking. He could also sleep on a book and remember its contents when he awoke.

CHAPTER 2

DISCOVER YOUR POWERS

Believe it or not, you were born psychic. Your abilities are part of your soul's adventures from the past. Throughout this chapter, you will learn how to dig deep into your memory and remember the psychic powers you may have had as a small child but that you may have gradually repressed as you entered adulthood. Rediscovering these memories will help you reclaim your unique psychic gifts, whether they include psychic dreams, near-death experiences, déjà vu, past-life influences, automatic writing, or other types of psychic intuition.

RECONNECT TO YOUR GIFTS

Psychic development begins at an early age. As a small child, you just used what came naturally to you. You didn't have to think about what you knew; you just knew, long before you became aware that not everyone knew the same way.

Can you remember your first psychic experience? Some of you can probably recall it clearly, while others may have little or no recognition of any psychic experience at all. Chances are that it came at a very early age. You may be able to find an older family member or acquaintance who can remember that you talked about some incident that you have consciously forgotten. It could have been a series of circumstances or a single event.

All of those past experiences are stored in your unconscious mind. Even as you read these words, you may call to mind something that you haven't thought about in years. Some of you may have powerful memories connected to "unexplainable experiences" in your past. As you progress through these pages, the goal is for you to be able to define and reconnect with your special psychic gifts.

Tips As You Try to Remember

Do you remember your early psychic experiences? Maybe you weren't aware at the time that what had occurred wasn't part of reality—that is, until you shared the information with others. Or maybe it was clearly a psychic event. Here are a few tips for trying to remember your early psychic experiences:

* Allow yourself to be open to recalling psychic memory flashes, and don't overanalyze them. These flashes may occur at any time as you progress through the book and practice the exercises.

* Don't expect to get all of the memory at once.

* Keep notes of your psychic memory flashes so that you can refer back to them.

✳ Once you have an idea of a possible psychic flash, talk to others who might have been aware of it at the time it happened.

✳ Use basic relaxation techniques to help you focus on your early psychic memories.

Exercise: Count to Remember Childhood Psychic Memories

Here is an easy relaxation exercise that may help you remember early childhood psychic memories. If you would like to try it, find a place to sit or lie down, and let yourself get comfortable.

> You may not be comfortable counting downward into an altered state of focus. Some people would rather feel themselves going upward or even walking through a hallway. If that is the case for you, consider reversing the numbers and counting from zero to five at the beginning and then counting down at the end of the exercise.

When you're ready, you may take a deep breath (again, at the level that is comfortable for you) and allow yourself to focus toward your third eye. As you breathe in and out, you may tell yourself that in a few moments you will count from five to zero. When you reach zero you will be very relaxed, and your unconscious mind will be open to recalling early childhood memories of psychic experiences. Any memory you may recall will be for positive insights, and at any time you want, you may always open your eyes and come back to full consciousness, refreshed and relaxed.

Count Down

As you count yourself down, you may feel yourself focusing more and more with each count. It is a very pleasant feeling, and you look forward to the next number. As you focus on your third eye, you may allow yourself to relax more and more as you open up your psychic memories. You may allow any muscles that you feel are stiff to relax. If you are ready, take a deep breath, exhale, and start counting.

Whenever you are connecting to your third eye, give yourself the suggestion that you may always end your connection by opening your eyes, taking a deep breath, and returning to a full state of consciousness completely aware of your surroundings, relaxed and refreshed.

* **5.**—Breathe in and out, and feel yourself relaxing more and more with each breath. Let yourself relax your muscles. As you mention the next number to yourself, you may feel yourself connecting more and more strongly with your third eye. You may feel yourself focusing on your unconscious mind, opening up to your early psychic memories.

* **4.**—Feel yourself entering into an altered state of focus as you feel the connection to your third eye becoming stronger and stronger. You may breathe in and out slowly, relaxing more and more with each breath. You may feel yourself getting closer and closer to your memories of your early psychic experiences.

* **3.**—As you breathe slowly, you may feel yourself relaxing more and more. You may feel yourself connecting more and more to your unconscious mind. As you get closer and closer to zero, you will be ready to focus on your early childhood psychic memories.

* **2.**—You are getting closer and closer. You are relaxing and your psychic memories will be ready for you to access when you get to

zero. As you breathe in and out slowly, you will allow yourself to relax more and more. You can feel your connection to your third eye more and more.

✳ **1.**—You are almost there. You may feel very comfortable, relaxed, and safe. You know you may always come back to a conscious state any time you want by opening your eyes, taking a deep breath, exhaling, and feeling relaxed and positive. You may allow yourself to go deeper and deeper as you count slowly backward from five to zero, each number ten times stronger than the last.

✳ **0.**—You may feel the connection to your third eye even more strongly than before, as you are now ready to access the unconscious memories of your early childhood experiences. Anything you see, feel, hear, taste, or smell will help you to remember these early psychic events.

While you are in a relaxed and comfortable state, you may let your unconscious memory recall images from the past about your early psychic experiences at a pace that is good and comfortable for you. Be aware that you can open your eyes and come back to full consciousness any time you want, feeling relaxed, calm, and refreshed.

Count Back Up

When you are ready, you may count slowly back up to your conscious mind. When you reach five, you will remember any images you may have recalled relating to early psychic experiences.

✳ **1.**—You are coming up and slowly releasing your connection to the third eye as you count toward five.

✳ **2.**—Breathe slowly and comfortably as you count yourself back up.

✳ **3.**—You are getting closer and closer to the surface of your conscious mind.

✳ **4.**—Slowly release your connection to the third eye.

✳ **5.**—Now you may come fully back to the surface of your conscious mind as you release your connection to the third eye. Take a deep breath, open your eyes, and exhale. You may feel relaxed and positive about your connection to any early childhood psychic memories that you may have recalled.

Each time you perform this exercise, you may have different results. Don't expect a specific outcome. Each time you try, you may find more and different memories coming up to the surface of your conscious mind. Once you open the communication channel and continue to connect to it, the flow will become easier to access.

NEAR-DEATH EXPERIENCES

Have you ever had a near-death experience? Was there ever a close call during which you were inches or moments away from potential death? Did you survive a bad fall or a blow to the head? Did you have other traumatic experiences when you were young in which your mind was an important key to your survival?

Near-death experiences come in many different ways, but going through such an experience may have "jump-started" your third eye into being more open to psychic intuition.

When you go through a traumatic experience, all of your senses experience a surge in the intensity of the power of their perception. In some cases, your view of the world changes dramatically. You know something's different, but you're not sure what it is.

A near-death experience in early childhood may often go unnoticed. Kids get into all kinds of trouble. They fall from trees, get trapped under water, trip down the stairs, survive a car accident, or tumble off the playground swings. In some cases, such a close call may grow out of an unconscious need to escape a traumatic situation, such as abuse or an emotionally unstable family.

Can you think of events in your life that may have affected your psychic ability? You are the sum of your life to this very moment. Each new, passing moment will bring about change. As you grow in your psychic awareness, you are actually getting back in tune with the abilities you were born with.

CHILDHOOD EXPERIENCES OF PSYCHIC INTUITION

The dreams you had in your childhood could very well have been psychic in nature. Dreams, like other psychic experiences, may deal with past events or future events, or they may provide insight into situations that are occurring at the time of the dream. Dreams are a great way to receive psychic information because the conscious analytical mind is at rest, and you are open to communication from your unconscious and your Universal Mind.

Think about the dreams you had as a child. Do you remember any? If so, ask yourself these questions:

* Can you recall if your dreams had a theme?

* Did you have a certain dream that occurred over and over?

* Can you identify the historical time period and/or location of any dreams?

* Did you have symbolic dreams that may not have made sense when you had them but that you might better understand at this point in your life?

* Did you have any dreams that identified situations in your life before you experienced them?

* Did you have recurring nightmares?

* Did you have dreams that were different but followed a related theme?

✳ Did you have dreams in which dead relatives or others who had passed over communicated with you?

✳ Did you have angels, guides, or other beings or animals come to you in your sleep to comfort you and/or offer you advice?

✳ Did you ever have dreams of flying or going to places that you had never been before?

✳ Do you recall any other types of dreams from childhood that may have been of a psychic nature?

You can investigate the answers to these questions in a relaxed state as you connect with your inner knowing through your third eye. Trust your intuitive mind to give you the right answers. You may not remember any of the dreams you had as a child, and that is okay. Dreams are only one way to connect to your natural psychic ability.

Second Sight in Childhood

"Second sight" is a term associated with the ability to perceive information through nontraditional or paranormal means. It could be the ability to psychically know events before they happen, or to see spirits, or to even be familiar with a location before actually visiting it. Perhaps you can remember experiences you have had in your life that indicate that you may have the gift of second sight.

When you were a child, did you ever see things that were invisible to others? Did you have "imaginary friends" to play with? Could you find your way to or around a place where you had never been before?

Can you recall any other experiences that you may have had as a child that may seem odd to you now? Did you ever have a visit from fairies or guides? Do you recall any contacts that could be considered otherworldly, such as with beings from another planet? If you think of one experience, then there's a good chance you may recall others.

A Sense of Déjà Vu

Déjà vu is the awareness that you have had an experience before even though you are doing something for the first time. It is like being in a time warp and watching yourself take part in the action unfolding around you. This experience can be confusing, or even disorienting, when it catches you by surprise.

Did you ever, as a child, go to a strange place and know you had been there before? Did you experience something and feel that it had already happened? Childhood déjà vu is a phenomenon that can happen naturally. As a child, your view of reality is different because your early psychic experiences aren't limited by the boundaries that society has set for adults.

Sometimes déjà vu is so strong that second sight engages, and the experience becomes so real that the person having the experience loses touch with reality. This happens to a child more easily than to an adult, but such an experience often stays with a child into adulthood.

Recalling Past Lives

Past-life memories come with you from lifetime to lifetime. They are housed in your unconscious mind, and they influence your life, even though you may not be aware of them. Many people go through their entire lives without understanding why they think or act the way they do. Your adult conscious mind often dismisses what children accept without question.

During childhood, you may still have memories from your past lives; these memories are gradually forgotten as you grow older. Do you recall any early childhood memories that can give you clues about your past lives? Did you know things about family members from different lifetimes? Did you ever act as if your role in the family was different than it should have been? Did you ever tell your family stories about other lifetimes?

Chances are, some of your psychic intuitions have come from what you've retained from your past. The more of these soul memories you can recall, the more you will find a connection to your psychic gifts.

Other Psychic Talents

When you were a child, did you have a natural talent for doing something? Did anyone ever remark that a particular ability of yours seemed developed far beyond your age? Did it seem as if you knew how to do something without anyone else showing you? Did you have a special athletic talent?

Your psychic talents may go beyond sight and hearing, although these are the more common senses for psychic power or recollection. Some of you may remember being able to sense energy fields or auras, or certain smells. And some of you may have at times felt unexplained emotions that had no real-life explanations.

Did you draw or paint at an early age? If so, were these scenes from your childhood, or did they seem to be inspired by something you had never actually experienced in this lifetime? Did you have a musical talent? Were there music styles or certain compositions that affected you in different ways?

Do you remember hearing voices? Did you have a guide or an angel who talked you through bad times and gave you encouragement? Or did the voice seem to come from an object you held dear—a doll, a baby blanket, or even your favorite chair?

RECLAIM YOUR PSYCHIC GIFTS

Now that you have had an opportunity to examine your childhood experiences of psychic intuition, think of how these gifts may be reclaimed and made a part of your present life. Some of you may use your intuitive abilities daily, and some of you may not, but it's never too late to reawaken your psychic powers. It is possible that you may be a little leery of getting in touch with your gifts. Remember that they are a natural part of your total self, no different than your physical body.

When you think back over your life and consider how some of your experiences may have been much more psychic than previously thought, you may have identified a correlation between these incidences that have been with you since birth. Granted, some of your "knowings" may not be to your liking. You may have tried to block out of your mind the ones that foretold of unpleasant outcomes in the future or the feeling of someone else's pain. Many people have grown up with the fear that they caused what they saw in their mind's eye.

You may have felt like an "outcast" growing up when you realized you were different from your friends and family. You may have even been ridiculed or bullied because you were misunderstood. Perhaps you were told never to share the psychic insights you were receiving so that you would not stand out from the norm.

The hope is that a new understanding of psychic abilities will evolve, an understanding that finally helps and encourages people to learn to use the nature of their being. There is no one on exactly the same frequency as you, and yet you, like everyone else, are connected to all matter. The exercises in this book are designed to help you understand your frequency and to learn to use your connection to develop your psychic abilities. As you practice, remember the incredible energy that the heart generates as you experience the Universe's unconditional love.

CHAPTER 3

STAY BALANCED AND CONNECTED

One of the most significant aspects of your psychic growth is developing the ability to keep yourself grounded or balanced. To do that, it is important to work with your fears and discover the support of your Belief (a divinity or higher power whose existence you believe in, whether because of your religion or personal conviction). At the end of the chapter, you will learn an exercise for surrounding yourself with the protective, unconditionally loving energy of the Universe and how to keep yourself connected.

WORK WITH YOUR FEARS AND DOUBTS

Opening up to your psychic ability can be overwhelming if you are not prepared. This problem is especially evident in children and teenagers. Their first encounters usually happen without warning, and they are left confused and afraid of the unknown. Many spend the rest of their lives trying to run away from their natural gifts.

For example, as a child, Pat was confronted in her house by an energy that visited her in her bedroom at night. Her parents had little sympathy for her fears. They insisted that it was all in her mind. Eventually she learned to block out the energy for the most part, but she still lived in fear of it returning when she least expected it until she learned that it was her psychic ability that had actually attracted the energy. Now she knows how to protect or ground herself.

It is very easy when you first start developing your psychic gifts to become overwhelmed with what you encounter. If that happens, you need to stop and take a deep breath, release it, and go back to a nonpsychic activity.

Internal Self-Doubt

Opening yourself up to self-doubt can lead to confusion. The doubt begins when you do not have a clear belief that your psychic abilities have been given to you for the good of the Universe. You can create the doubt in yourself, or others can create the doubt in you.

Often, self-doubt is the result of fear. It is in your human nature to try to avoid the unknown, which by nature includes some potentially dangerous situations. But when you run from fear, it follows you and grows in proportion to your retreat. Most often you are afraid without knowing what you are afraid of. It is this fear of the unknown that can paralyze your psychic development.

In his book *The Gift of Fear*, Gavin de Becker indicates that when you fight fear, it becomes part of your family. In other words, the fear lives with you all the time. When you stop and ask yourself what your fear really is, you are taking an important step, not only in beginning to understand how it is affecting you but in finding ways to successfully deal with it.

Fear of the unknown can eat away at your whole being. It can prevent you from moving forward along your life map. It can bring you face to face with old unresolved karma. Fear can rear its ugly head at any moment. It can manifest itself through your unconscious mind.

The Influence of Others

Equally damaging is advice from well-meaning people who are consumed by their own fears. If you confide in them, these people may tell you that your psychic gifts are weird or even evil. They are quick to advise you about something they do not understand. The fears of others are just as toxic to you as your own—they will contribute to your own fears and may smother your psychic gifts.

A negative reaction can increase your self-doubt. As long as you let yourself be open to the fears of other people, you run the danger of internalizing them. An unbalanced and ungrounded person may absorb another person's fears instantly, losing self-confidence and replacing it with self-doubt.

As you learn how to ground yourself and find your balance, you will be able to react to fear in a different way. You will learn to move aside and get out of the line of fire of other people's fears. You can find security in your psychic intuition and learn to trust your personal guidance system. You can replace doubt with trust.

STAY FOCUSED

Have you ever looked at a multiple-image hologram? A multiple-image hologram is a picture that contains two (usually contrasting) images. If you stare at the one, you won't be able to see the other. The key is for you not to focus on what you are looking at until the second image emerges from the first. Some second images are easy to see as you turn the picture. Others pictures require that you let your eyes go out of focus until you see the second image. Some of you may not be able to see two distinct pictures. Inversely, some of you may see two images in a picture that has only one.

Focus on the Big and Little Picture

There are two ways to focus the mind: the big picture and the little picture. As with a multiple-image hologram, if you focus on only one image, you may fail to see the other. When you focus on fear and self-doubt, you may fail to see love and the strength of the Universe. When you fail to separate your role from that of the whole Universe, you can lose focus of your own life map.

If you can see only the big picture, you are detaching yourself from your inner guidance system. You may be keeping yourself at such a distance that you are unable to take an active role in the work of the Universe. It is possible that you will not take the risk of self-improvement even though you know that is what you need to do. This inaction may cause you to feel paralyzed and unable to get on track with your life map.

When you see only the little picture, you become responsible for all of the Universe's work. You keep repeating karmic patterns over and over again and fail to see how you have an opportunity to learn, grow, and change. You are weighed down with the responsibility of not only solving your own problems but everyone else's, too. If you are like this, then you already know that others will constantly bombard you with their problems. They leave feeling better while you are left cleaning up their mess.

FIND YOUR BELIEF

To help you keep grounded and in balance, you can count on some help. If you participate in an organized religion, you can rely on the divinity or divinities of that Belief System. In fact, many psychics belong to an organized religion. Your psychic ability is a part of your soul, as ancient as any religion. God, as that being is understood by most modern religions, is a part of all that is good. The Divine works for the betterment of humankind—that is, God's role is that of the Universal Mind.

It is also possible that you cannot define exactly what you believe. It may be that you see God as a part of nature—the oceans, forests, mountains, and all living things on the earth and in the sky. That is okay as long as you believe that there is a positive force, somewhere in the Universe, that watches over you and others. Whoever that being or higher power is, that is your Belief.

Can You Identify Your Belief?

If you do not have an organized religion, what or whom do you believe in? Do you believe that there is a Divinity somewhere in the Universe? Do you believe that you have a soul? Do you believe in the powers of good and evil? Do you believe that you have a purpose in life?

Can you define your Belief in your own words? Take a few moments to consider your answers. How would you explain your Belief to anyone else? How comfortable are you defining your Belief?

Do you believe in miracles? And if you do, how often are you aware of them happening around you? Are you aware of them daily or only occasionally?

Remember that it's okay not to have definite answers for these questions. These questions are merely here to help you become aware of and work toward identifying your Belief. Your Belief is already inside you. You were born with it, and all your actions and thoughts are either in tune with it or not.

Here are some further questions to think about in terms of your Belief:

* Do you rely on angels, saints, or other beings to work their good?

* Do you look to something to protect you from both the known and the unknown? Can you turn there when you are faced with an unknown fear?

* Do you communicate with your Belief on a daily basis, just when you remember to, or only at times when you are asking for something?

* Do you feel that you and this higher power are compatible and in tune with each other, or do you feel as if you are in conflict?

Exercise: Contemplate Your Belief

Here is an exercise to help you contemplate your Belief. If you choose to try it, take a few moments to get comfortable; then allow yourself to take a deep breath, exhale, and relax. You may count yourself down from five to zero and feel yourself connected to your inner guidance system. (Each time you relax, it is always different—sometimes in a deep focus and sometimes not.)

As you count yourself down, you may suggest that with each count you will feel more and more relaxed and in tune with your third eye and your inner guidance system. You may allow yourself to feel a connection to your Belief, whether you know exactly what it is or not. If you are still unsure, then allow yourself to be open to the positive flow of the Universe. When you reach zero, give yourself some time to feel a positive connection to your Belief. If you have concerns for yourself or others or for the development of your psychic gifts, you may turn them over to your Belief for resolution and guidance.

After you have spent some time contemplating your Belief, you may take a deep breath, exhale, and count yourself slowly upward to five and the surface of your mind. When you get back to five, take another breath, exhale, and come back to your conscious mind. It is okay to include this communication in your daily relaxation exercises.

Anchor Your Connection

You can give yourself a mental or physical anchor while you are relaxed and connected to your Belief. Put your thumb and forefinger together and squeeze lightly. As you do this, you may suggest to yourself that whenever you repeat this action, you will feel connected to your Belief. The level of connection will always be at the focus level, which is positive and aware. In other words, if you are driving a car, you will always be alert and awake when you trigger your anchor.

The same effect can be obtained if you use a verbal anchor. A verbal anchor may be a specific word as simple as "Believe." Other types of anchors may be auditory (a specific sound), olfactory (a certain smell), or mental (the memory of a particular smell). It could even be the positive feeling you get when you are in a special place.

An anchor is a neurolinguistic programming (NLP) word for the process of recalling and experiencing a suggestion given while in a relaxed altered state of focus. A touch or keyword is introduced and practiced so that when it is used after the trance state has ended, the same result will be experienced again. NLP anchoring techniques can bring about positive changes by installing new positive mental images in the unconscious mind.

An anchor is a way to instantly experience a positive connection to your Belief. The more you practice making this connection, the easier it will be for you to make. If you consciously practice triggering your anchors, you will begin to do it automatically within a short period of time. The more comfortable you become communicating with your Belief, the more confidence you will have in it.

It is possible that you may already be using negative anchors, probably without any conscious awareness on your part at all. They can trigger your self-doubt. When you are connected to your psychic ability, a negative anchor may trigger and bring back an old fear or doubt. If this is the case for you, then you may use your positive belief anchor to reframe a negative one.

One concept of NLP is that the brain is like a computer—it operates on the program that has been installed in it unless a different program is installed. A "reframe" is the installation of a new mental program. This is accomplished when the unconscious mind is open to the new suggestion.

CONNECT WITH YOUR BELIEF

Once you have become comfortable communicating with your Belief, you are ready to begin working with it. To begin, this means establishing a communication connection that can either remain open or be opened instantly, whenever you wish, by triggering your belief anchor(s). Your Belief is part of your inner guidance system, and when you are open to its communication, you are also working with your psychic abilities.

For those of you grounded in the Christian faith, do you know what the centermost verse in the Bible is? It is Psalm 118:8, and it states, "It is better to trust in the Lord than to put confidence in man."

As you develop a partnership with your Belief, you will also become more in tune with your life purpose. This partnership is necessary for your life work—what you do during your lifetime that provides an opportunity for humankind to benefit in ways that help you and others progress along their life maps.

A great way to connect with your Belief instantly is to go through your third eye. Just feel the vibration in the middle of your forehead and believe. Take a deep breath, and exhale to add to a relaxed positive state. It is something you can do any time. No one around you will be aware of it, except perhaps another psychic who may be observing your aura.

Add Some Love

Love is a very powerful emotion that you can use to help you solidify your connection to your Belief. First, think of something or someone that represents unconditional love. It might be a person, an animal, or an action, such as simply helping someone. It may be a feeling that you have not had often in your life or one that you experience every day.

Imagine that the force in the Universe that watches over you represents the feeling of unconditional love. That love is not judgmental; it is just there to support you. It also represents a powerful force whose purpose is to stand guard over your fears.

Now try adding the feeling of love to your third-eye connection. Take a deep breath and feel yourself shifting your focus to your third eye. As you breathe in and out, feel unconditional love flowing through your body. Feel the protective strength that goes with that love. When you are ready, change your focus back to your conscious mind, returning with the positive feeling of that unconditional love that is watching over you.

CREATE A PROTECTIVE BUBBLE

You can do the following exercise to create a bubble of protection around you that can help you find and maintain your balance to keep you grounded. This bubble comes through your Belief. It can help you dissociate and step back to get the whole view of any situation that you find yourself in or need to address. If you are ready to try it, find a comfortable place, take a deep breath, exhale, and allow yourself to relax. You may first try this exercise by counting down or up. However, as you learn how to develop an anchor, you can connect with your protective bubble any time you want by just changing your focus.

Once you become comfortable with your protective bubble, it can become part of your partnership with the Universal Mind and a powerful tool to keep you grounded and in balance. This bubble may be any color you would like—most people use a golden imagery or a clear positive energy. It can give you the feeling of being wrapped in a beautiful secure blanket, just as you may have experienced as a child.

There are several ways in which you can experience the protective bubble exercise. You may read it out loud to yourself, memorize it, have someone else read it to you, or record it and play it back to yourself.

The protective bubble exercise is designed to help you develop a safe and secure feeling in your Belief. You are free to incorporate any image that helps you reach that state.

Exercise: Create a Bubble of Protection

As you breathe slowly in and out, you may be aware that you have many muscles throughout your body. Some are tight and some are loose. Each time you feel a muscle stiffen, you may relax it, and as you are doing so, you may relax more and more. You may be aware of different muscles stiffening and relaxing as you experience this protective bubble exercise.

Feel yourself connecting to your third eye as you slowly focus on your breathing. You may be aware of different sounds around you. You may notice that you have many different thoughts coming into your head, and if so, that's okay. You may feel your third eye as it is connected to your Universal Mind and as it opens to the Universal Flow. As you count yourself down, feel the protective bubble surround you and flow over your body:

* **5.**—You may feel and see in your mind's eye a beautiful golden light that starts to flow through your third eye and down over your forehead, your face, and the back of your head. It flows all the way down to your neck. It is a wonderful, secure, and loving energy filled with all the positive vibrations of the Universe.

* **4.**—You may now feel the loving energy of your protective bubble flowing over your shoulders, down your arms to your elbows, down your forearms and wrists, and over your fingertips. It is a wonderfully relaxing, safe, and secure feeling. You feel the energy of the Universe flowing through and over and around your head, shoulders, arms, and fingers. As you slowly breathe in and out and feel the Universal Flow, you will go deeper and deeper into a safe, secure, and relaxed state.

* **3.**—You may feel your protective bubble spreading slowly down over your chest to your waist. You may feel it as it flows over the upper half of your body, wrapping you in a beautiful secure blanket of golden light. As you breathe slowly in and out, you will become more and more comfortable with this loving flow of the Universe.

* **2.**—You may feel your protective bubble spreading over your thighs to your knees. You are in a beautiful and secure capsule of Universal Love and positive energy. Breathe slowly in and out, and you will relax more and more as you focus on your connection to the Universal Mind.

✳ **1.**—You may feel your protective bubble flow over you all the way down from your third eye to your ankles. You are almost totally immersed in the love and positive energy of the Universe. You feel comfortable, safe, and secure as you focus more and more on the positive energy in your protective bubble.

✳ **0.**—You are now totally surrounded by your protective bubble sent to you from the Universal Mind. You may feel this loving energy flow going through your whole body and surrounding you. Take a few moments and enjoy this beautiful, loving energy.

Protection for the Mind, Body, and Soul

While you are in this beautiful and secure state, allow yourself to feel the loving energy of the Universe as it wraps you in a protective bubble. You may communicate with your Divinity, saints, or other positive religious beliefs. You may feel at this time that you are not alone in your journey through your life map, and you may know that your Universal team will be with you to help and guide you every step of your way.

If you have any worries or questions for the Universal Mind, you may ask that you receive the proper help and guidance. You may ask that you will be given the proper tools to help stay in tune with your life map. You may request that the Universal loving energy protect you against the forces that would control your mind, your body, and your soul. You may ask that you receive protection against any other who would use his or her psychic gifts against you.

Many beginning psychics can be startled when they first release themselves into the Universal Flow. As long as you have a connection to where you are, you will return safely. In other words, you will always know where the "ground" is.

You may cloak yourself in your protective bubble as you become more in tune with your psychic gifts. You may open to the Universe's guidance for the proper development and use of your psychic abilities. You may feel safe and protected by the Universe's loving energy as you give permission for your psychic gifts to be developed and used in a way that is good for humankind. Take a few moments as you breathe slowly in and out and feel the love and positive energy that flows over and around you.

You may give yourself a keyword or physical anchor to help you connect to your bubble at any moment you want or need to. While you are still in your protected state, try out your anchors. Practice focusing on your third eye and instantly feel the Universe's loving energy start to flow. Take one more moment to feel your special connection and then slowly count yourself back up to five, opening your eyes and feeling relaxed, calm, positive, full of Universal Love, and protected by your own personal bubble.

Maintain a Connection

While you're immersed in this Universal Energy, it is very natural to feel as if you can float up into the Universe. In fact, you may begin to experience yourself lifting out of your body. If you're not prepared, it can be unsettling. Similar experiences have turned away many first-time psychic floaters. As you learned earlier in the chapter, the unknown can create a lot of fear.

As you feel yourself filling with the Universe's loving energy, also see and feel a golden thread that extends down from the Universe and that is firmly anchored to the earth through you. This thread is strong enough to tether you and the bubble that surrounds you to the ground. You may feel secure and safe if you begin to float up into the Universe because you will know that you can always follow the golden thread back to your place on earth.

As you progress in your psychic development, you may want to review the material in this chapter from time to time so that you may remind yourself of your Belief and the safety of your protective bubble. Your life may be full of little bumps and turns. Staying grounded will help you navigate along your life map.

CHAPTER 4

GET IN TOUCH WITH YOUR ABILITIES

Just as your physical genetic makeup is unique, so is your mental makeup. Understanding your mental makeup will help you communicate better, not only with yourself but also with others. You will be able to explain your own mind and understand how someone else's mental makeup works. This will help you get your message across more easily and more effectively. In this chapter, you will learn about your mental makeup and how your particular mind processes the input you receive through your five senses. By identifying your mental strengths, you can use them to enter an altered state of focus and conduct other exercises that will help you get in touch with your intuitive abilities.

USE YOUR SENSES

You have five different ways in which you experience the world around you. You see, you hear, you feel (both by touch and emotion), you taste, and you smell. As you consider how you process information through your senses, you may find that you rely on one input more than another. You may be very strong in one sensory area and weak in another. Understanding how your mind works can be a great asset in advancing your psychic development. Remember, there is no one else like you. You are unique and special, and your psychic images will be different than everyone else's.

Exercise: Explore Your Five Senses

To help you figure out what senses work best for you, you may try the following sense imagery exercises. You can try them with a friend or a small group if you wish. After you are done, you can compare among yourselves the differences in your responses.

As you identify your mental makeup, take note of the positive images you can produce. These images can be an aid in strengthening your altered state of focus. The more you allow yourself to experience the positive feelings that they generate, the more focused on your abilities you will become.

Your Sense of Vision

Most people are visual. Let's find out if you are, too. When you are ready, find a comfortable place, take a deep breath, exhale, and focus on your third eye, that spot in the middle of your forehead above your eyes. Once you are in a comfortable, relaxed, altered state of focus, consider the following exercise.

Think back to a pleasant memory in your life. If for some reason nothing comes to mind, you can always imagine something pleasant. Try to picture images of this event in your mind.

* Are the images in color, black and white, or somewhere in between?

* Are they clear, bright, and in focus, or are they unclear and out of focus?

* Can you change the picture, such as seeing it in a different time, either in the past or in the future?

* Do you see it as a movie or as a still photograph?

* Can you rewind a moving picture in your mind and watch it again, or stop it and focus on a single frame?

* Can you move the picture, bring it closer, push it farther away, or change the angle?

* Can you view it from above or from a lower position?

* Can you see yourself in the picture?

* Can you see the picture without seeing yourself?

* Can you see yourself at a different age, either younger or older?

* Can you see colors around people in your imagination?

* Can you see energy forms or other elements in your mind?

There are two types of visual images: experienced and dissociated. "Dissociate" means to be apart from the picture without feeling any emotions in connection with it. Some people can dissociate from an image in their mind, and some people cannot. It is good for you to know your image ability as you work on psychic development.

Your Sense of Hearing

Next, you can examine your sense of hearing. You may use your same pleasant memory from the past.

* Can you imagine sounds in your head? If so, what are they?

* Can you imagine music or sounds of nature, such as birds singing or the sounds of the ocean? Can you turn the volume up or down in your mind?

* Can you see a picture in your mind and hear the sounds that go with it?

* Can you put yourself in the picture image and move around and hear sounds or conversations from different locations?

* Can you watch the image as if it were a movie or a video and still be able to hear the sound?

Additionally you may ask yourself these questions:

* Can you hear conversations taking place in your mind?

* Can you hear your own voice?

* Do these voices you can hear talk to you, and are they part of something other than yourself?

* Can you have a discussion with a voice in your head?

If you have voices in your mind that are persistently negative and create bad thoughts for you, you should seek out a licensed mental health professional in your area for proper guidance.

Your Sense of Feeling

Your sense of feeling is called the kinesthetic sense. You experience your kinesthetic information in two different ways: internally, as an emotional process, and externally, as a tactile or touch experience.

✳ First of all, can you imagine any emotions connected to your pleasant memory from the past? If so, can you feel these positive feelings now?

✳ Have you ever experienced feelings such as happiness, loneliness, or sadness in your mind? Can you intensify and weaken these emotions at will?

✳ Can you imagine visual pictures that create emotional feelings in yourself?

✳ Can you disconnect your emotions from the images in your mind? Can you step in and out of the scene, feeling and then not feeling the emotions connected to it, as you wish?

✳ Can you feel the emotions of different people when you are in their presence or when you remember them or see a picture of them?

✳ Is it easy to be overcome by emotional images that you mentally experience?

✳ Do you connect emotions to certain sounds or music?

✳ Do you feel emotions in certain places or objects?

✳ Can you connect sights, sounds, and emotional feelings in the same image?

✳ Can you imagine feeling positive or negative, or feeling healing energy in your mind's images?

✳ Can you imagine positive energies going through your body?

* Can you feel energy in terms of certain colors?

* Can you put yourself inside one of your mental images and imagine feeling temperatures, textures, and the weight of different objects?

* Could you imagine looking through the eyes of someone else and feeling the length of her hair or the texture of the clothes she is wearing?

* Can you combine emotions and your sense of touch?

* Can you connect your kinesthetic sense to your visual and hearing senses? Can you dissociate and watch and hear a visual and sound image, and yet feel the emotions and certain touches?

* Can you step in and out of the image and see, hear, and feel it in your mind?

Your Senses of Smell and Taste

Returning to your positive visual memory from the past, can you imagine any smells in your mind? Can you put yourself in that picture and move around, and experience different smells? Can you intensify or weaken smells in your mind? Can you imagine a favorite relaxing smell? If so, take a moment and just experience it.

You don't need to count yourself down when you practice sensory imagery, but you can develop a scent anchor that will help you go into a light trance by recalling the smell and taking a deep breath of it. You can also use your third eye to help you focus on and enhance a clearer image.

Do you have a favorite food? If so, can you imagine the taste? Perhaps you have a food that you do not like. Is it the taste, the smell, the feel, or the way it looks that bothers you? Are there certain tastes of food that bring you back to earlier pleasant memories in your life?

Can you connect smells with emotional feelings, or with sounds, foods, nature, or other mind images? Can you connect smells and tastes? Can you picture foods and connect tastes with them? Can you imagine eating a meal and tasting the different ingredients? Can you feel different emotions connected to different tastes?

CREATE AN ALTERED STATE OF FOCUS

Now that you have explored how your sensory imagery recall works and what senses work best for you, it is time to learn how to do some relaxation exercises to enhance your altered state of focus. This exercise is designed for you to count yourself to a place where you feel the positive Universal Energy that flows through your connection to the Universal Mind. It is in that place and through your third eye that you are connected with the Universe. Through this connection, you may use your sensory images to develop and bring into focus your natural psychic abilities.

This exercise is designed to help you use your sense imagery to build an even stronger link through your third eye to your unconscious and your Universal Mind. By anticipating and recalling a positive memory experience, you put yourself in your "comfort zone." This process also helps sharpen your focus on something that is positive and relaxing.

The more you focus on the image of a positive, relaxing experience, the more you open yourself to the Universal Energy. Your psychic gifts are a natural part of this process. As you allow them to be open to the Universal Flow, you will get psychic messages that are much clearer.

Exercise: How to Create an Altered State

If you practice a simple exercise like this every day, you may be amazed at how it can help you relax and stay in balance. It is also helpful in conditioning your mind to enhance altered states of consciousness that are comfortable and positive.

To begin, you may loosen your clothing and find a comfortable place to sit or lie down. Now, think of your favorite relaxing place. You may have a special place that you like to go to in your unconscious mind. This may be an actual place from earlier in your life, or it may be a place you currently enjoy. It could be an image of an activity or a sport that you enjoy experiencing or watching. It could be reading or watching television. Anything positive that you can feel can help enhance your focus.

When you focus on a familiar and positive image, you are much more receptive to it. The more you accept its reality, the better you will be able to focus on the image. This process is like priming a pump. Once information starts to reach you, it will flow easier and easier.

This place could be outside or inside, real or imagined—a place that is calm, relaxing, positive, and safe. If your mind works well with the sense of hearing, imagine relaxing sounds that you would hear in this place. If it would be helpful, you may also add feelings, tastes, and smells to your mind's image.

Your comfortable place in your mind may have originated in your dreams or from another source. You may not even have an image at all, just a feeling deep inside yourself. You may see colors or feel energy or hear a relaxing sound. A relaxing smell can be a major factor in helping you develop your psychic altered state of consciousness.

Incorporate Your Senses

As you focus on your breathing, imagine that you are inhaling your favorite relaxing smell. If you want, you can use an actual smell such as incense or a candle to help you connect with your breathing. You may remind yourself that each time you experience the smell of this relaxing aroma, you will enjoy it more and more.

If you have a favorite relaxing color, you may imagine that and add it to your breathing by feeling the peaceful energy every time you inhale and exhale. You may also imagine your favorite relaxing music or sounds as you breathe in and out. You may feel positive waves of energy flowing throughout your body with each slow, comfortable breath you take. You may feel your muscles relaxing as these waves flow through and over you.

You may picture your image in color as full and beautiful as you can imagine. You may watch your image, or you may step into it, experiencing all its relaxing feelings. You may move around in your image and experience many different things. You may sit back and enjoy yourself as if you were being entertained at a play or movie. Just enjoy yourself for a few moments, and when you're ready, take a deep breath and open your eyes, feeling relaxed and positive.

USING AN ALTERED STATE TO CONNECT TO PSYCHIC ABILITIES

Now that you are able to go into a comfortable altered state of focus, you can use it to help you develop your psychic abilities. As you step into your focused state, you can combine your sensory image strengths that are part of your natural mental makeup with your third eye and your Belief and guidance systems.

Exercise: Connect to Your Abilities

If you experience this exercise daily, it can have a powerful and positive effect on your life. This exercise can help you develop your psychic abilities as well as give you balance in the rest of your daily life by helping you deal with the challenges and resistances you face. As you perform this exercise, remember that your way of making this connection is unique, and no one else will experience it the same way.

Create a Script

Certain techniques can assist you into your psychic altered state of focus. You may want to create a set of directions, often called a script. Using a script can give you a consistent way of connecting to your psychic abilities.

You can write out your script if you want and make changes to it as you repeat the exercise. You can record it, or you might choose to have someone read it to you. At first you may want to work on only one portion at a time, at least until you get comfortable with each section. You can always use aids, such as recorded music or other sounds that help induce a trance for you. The more you practice, the easier it will be to enter a deeper state of relaxation.

Prepare Yourself

This exercise could take ten to twenty minutes to complete. You may want to plan a time when you are likely to have the fewest interruptions. This may help you enhance and develop your altered state of focus. If there are others who might try to interrupt, you might consider asking them to help by giving you this period of uninterrupted time.

Start the exercise by taking in a deep breath of your favorite relaxing smell, if you have one, and slowly exhaling. As you continue to breathe in and out slowly, let your eyes and mind focus upward to your third eye. When you're ready, let your eyes close as you feel the connection to your third eye becoming stronger and stronger. Let yourself drift farther and farther away from your surroundings while still knowing where you are.

Spend a few moments just enjoying this experience as you feel the protective bubble of the Universe surrounding you with loving energy. You may let your muscles relax as you breathe in and out. You may imagine your favorite sounds and smells and let them help you relax even more. Any conscious thoughts you have may come and go without resistance as you allow yourself to relax in this loving energy.

If for some reason an exercise makes you uncomfortable, just open your eyes and return to full consciousness feeling relaxed and positive. Then you can feel free to resume your daily activities. You may also remind yourself that you will go to an altered state of focus that is right for the moment, and in this state you will be aware of your surroundings.

Counting Down

You may now feel your third-eye connection to the protective bubble of loving energy from the Universe as it prepares to spread over your body. You may feel very positive and relaxed as you enjoy its protective energy. If you are ready, you may begin counting downward from five to zero, or upward from zero to five, as you prepare to experience a pleasant memory image in all your five senses. It may be the same image every time or a different one, real or imaginary:

✳ **5.**—Take a deep breath and feel the loving energy from the Universe begin to spread down over your third eye and your forehead, eyes, nose, cheeks, the back of your head, mouth, chin, and neck, to your shoulders. You may feel yourself sinking deeper and deeper as though you were descending a stairway to the center of your unconscious and through to your Universal Mind. With each step, you will focus more and more as your connection gets stronger and stronger.

✳ **4.**—You may now feel the loving energy spread over your shoulders and down your upper arms, your elbows, forearms, wrists, and fingers, all the way to the fingertips. As you breathe in and out, you may feel yourself focusing more and more. You may experience the protective energy of the Universe.

✳ **3.**—You may feel the loving energy spread down over the upper part of your body, over your chest and back, and all the way to your waist. You may feel yourself wrapped in this protective bubble of Universal Energy. You may focus on your favorite sound or smell as you slowly breathe in and out. You feel your third eye and the connection to the Universe getting stronger and stronger as you feel the power of the positive protective energy that flows over you.

✳ **2.**—This positive energy is now spreading all the way down to your knees as you feel yourself relaxing more and more. Any positive imagery you experience is getting clearer and clearer as you focus on the beauty and powerful energy of the Universal Mind. You feel safe and protected, far away from the conscious world around you.

✳ **1.**—You are almost at that special place inside of your mind. You may feel the loving energy spreading down to your ankles as you relax more and more. You may feel your focus becoming clearer and clearer as you drift away from your conscious thoughts. The protective energy flows around and over you.

✳ **0.**—You are in a focused state of communication with the Universal Mind. You feel yourself totally wrapped in the protective, loving energy of the Universe. You feel safe and secure.

This is an excellent method to help you strengthen your focus. At zero, you can practice getting clear images in each one of the five senses. Try changing your perspective as you experience your image. The more comfortable you become, the more it will help your psychic development.

Develop Your Focus

Take a few moments to enjoy this protective energy of the Universe. When you are ready, focus on a positive visual image from either your memory or from your imagination. Allow this image to become clearer and clearer as you bring it into focus. You may add in your other senses, that is, your sense of hearing, feeling, taste, and smell. The more you experience, the more you will feel the powerful, protective energy of the Universal Mind. You are now wrapped in your protective bubble of Universal light.

Feel yourself moving about in your image. You may choose simply to watch, or you may experience all the positive sensations connected with it. Feel yourself totally connected to your Belief and all the Universal knowledge that is there to help and guide you. Breathe slowly in and out as you focus on your positive, relaxing images. You are far removed from your conscious, analytical mind.

Explore Your Senses

Let yourself focus in on your visual image. You may be able to see colors or energy. Put yourself in the image and move around the scene. Then watch it from a distance. Each time you experience it, you will see something that is important to focus on. Continue to breathe in and out, feeling relaxed and connected to the protective energy of the Universe.

Now focus on your hearing sense. Imagine sounds that are relaxing and positive. Turn the volume up or down, and slow the sounds down or speed them up. Adjust what you are hearing until the sounds are in the proper balance for you. The more comfortable you are, the more you will focus. If you can hear pleasant conversations going on within your image, let yourself listen in, and move about from different viewpoints.

Next, add in your kinesthetic sense to get the feel of the image and the moods. Experience different textures, temperatures, and emotions. Now include tastes and smells. Let yourself drift through a virtual reality of your different senses. Spend as long as you want there, feeling safe and secure as you explore the regions of your unconscious and your Universal Mind.

Anchor Your Experience

Before you leave and return to the surface of your conscious mind, give yourself word and touch anchors that will help you re-create your connection with your sense imagery. Choose a word that brings back this special feeling. Say it to yourself several times, experiencing how you feel when you are connected to your Universal Energy. Do the same thing with a touch, such as a thumb and finger pressed together.

While you are still in your relaxed state, suggest to yourself that each time you experience this exercise or use your anchors, you will become more and more comfortable with the way you process your five sense images. You may tell yourself that your abilities are given to you by the Universe to be used for the good of both yourself and others.

A suggestion to help you reach an altered state can be presented to your unconscious mind while it is in a relaxed state and free from your analytical conscious mind. When you present the suggestion in this way, you are adding it to your unconscious memory, and when you need to feel the suggestion, your anchor will help it surface in your conscious mind where it is accepted without question.

You may suggest that any time you need it, the Universe's bubble of loving energy is there to surround you and protect you. It is a suggestion you can use every day. This will be helpful as you experience the various psychic development exercises in the upcoming chapters of this book.

Back to the Surface

When you are ready, you may begin to count yourself back up to the surface of your conscious mind, from one to five:

✻ **1.**—You are relaxed and refreshed as you begin your journey back. Breathe in and out slowly and comfortably. All your tensions have disappeared.

✻ **2.**—You continue upward. The positive images and Universal Energy are still vivid in your mind. Your protective bubble accompanies you as you continue your journey back to consciousness. You feel so relaxed and positive.

✻ **3.**—You are halfway there. You look forward to bringing your experiences back to the surface to assist you as you move about the conscious world.

✻ **4.**—You can see the surface of your conscious mind just ahead. As you come to the last number, take a deep, comfortable, relaxing breath.

✻ **5.**—Exhale, open your eyes slowly, and come back to the surface of your conscious mind, relaxed, refreshed, and still filled with the loving energy of the Universe.

Take a few moments to readjust to the world about you. Keep this positive experience with you as you go on about your day or evening.

The more you are aware of how your mind works and processes your sense images, the more you will learn to trust and rely on them. These are the images that may have confronted you in the past when you were unprepared for them. Now you have the opportunity to examine and study them from your safe protective bubble of Universal loving energy. The more you use your positive anchors, the more you will begin to automatically sense this bubble all around you.

CHAPTER 5

UTILIZE YOUR CHAKRAS

Your chakras are the energy centers in your body, and much of your psychic information comes through them. The word "chakra" comes from the Sanskrit word for "wheel." Hindu and Buddhist religions believe that the human body has a series of energy centers that act as openings for Universal energies to pass through the body's aura. Like wheels, the chakras vibrate and turn at different speeds to help receive and distribute the energy. This chapter will help you examine seven major chakra centers of the human body. Then you will learn how to perform exercises that will help you open and balance these energy centers. Balanced chakras will help you in your psychic development.

YOUR PSYCHIC ENERGY

Energy is believed to be the basis of all matter. Under that principle, anything that can be transformed into pure energy can be transmitted through the dimensions of time. Perhaps you remember watching *Star Trek* on television. When Captain Kirk ordered, "Beam me up, Scotty!" he would dissolve into a shimmering mass of energy and be transported through space back to the *Enterprise*.

In a way, this is how psychic information is received—through transference of psychic energy. The psychic energy can be converted into images that may be processed through the five different senses: sight, sound, touch, taste, and smell. Having your chakra centers in tune and in balance helps the psychic energy flow through you.

Tibetan Buddhists see each chakra as a wheel with a different number of spokes. The energy level of each center turns its wheel at a different speed. Not all of the chakra models have seven energy centers. Some have more, and some have less.

When the chakra centers are blocked, the signal or energy will not come through. At the same time, when the centers are wide open, the flow may be so powerful that the psychic images become overpowering. Knowing when and how much to open your psychic energy flow is a delicate skill that is achieved with practice and patience.

Once you learn to keep your psychic equipment in good working order, you will be able to tune in with the confidence that you will receive an energy signal that can be trusted and relied on.

The Aura Field

A field of energy called an "aura" surrounds your body. If this field is interrupted for some reason, the energy will not flow evenly.

Your chakras are an essential part of this energy flow. If one or more of them is closed, then the energy is blocked at these points. Energy blocks throw your aura out of balance.

Blocked energy that is not cleared can lead to potentially serious consequences. This can affect your mental, physical, and spiritual health. Blocked energy can also severely impede your spiritual and psychic development. As you learn to tune your chakras, you will also balance your aura and advance your intuitive gifts.

Many psychics are able to perceive other people's auras. Some sense it visually, as colors or streaks of energy. Others may feel them physically or mentally. Each psychic interprets what he or she experiences differently.

THE SEVEN CHAKRA CENTERS

There are seven major chakra centers in the human body, as well as many minor ones. Note that each chakra center has a related endocrine gland that secretes hormones. The better your energy centers and your glands work together, the greater the opportunity is for your body, mind, and soul to be in harmony with one another.

The seven chakra centers are:

1. **The base, or root, chakra (Muladhara).** The lowest of the seven major centers, this chakra is located at the base of the spine and is the simplest of the seven. It relates to your physical strength and animalistic nature, as well as the senses of taste and smell. It is in the base chakra that the kundalini energy waits in coiled readiness to respond to your basic needs. (According to the yogis, kundalini energy is the psychospiritual energy that is a powerful source of many psychic experiences.) This chakra controls the gonads.

2. **The sacral, or belly, chakra (Svadhisthana).** Located just below the navel, near the genitals, the sacral chakra controls sexual energy and reproduction and may affect your health when out of balance. It influences how your pancreas and liver function.

This chakra also controls what is known as the cells of Leydig, testicular or ovarian cells that secrete testosterone.

3. **The solar-plexus chakra (Manipura).** Located below the breastbone and above the navel, the solar-plexus chakra is the center where mediums get their psychic information. The solar-plexus chakra controls the adrenal glands; when it is out of balance, it can affect your stomach, liver, and pancreas.

4. **The heart chakra (Anahata).** Located in the center of the chest and in the middle of your shoulder blades, the heart chakra relates to the Universal Mind and emotions such as love, honesty, and caring. If it becomes blocked, it can affect your heart, lungs, and breathing. It also rules your thymus gland.

5. **The throat chakra (Vishuddha).** Located at the top of the throat, the throat chakra relates to creativity, self-expression, and the creative arts, including music, art, and writing. When its center is blocked, your throat, ears, eyes, nose, and mouth may be affected. This chakra rules the thyroid gland.

6. **The forehead, or third-eye, chakra (Ajna).** Located between and above your two eyes in the center of your forehead, the forehead, or third-eye, chakra relates to your pituitary gland and your psychic ability. When this center is blocked, it can affect your head, eyes, and brain.

7. **The crown chakra (Sahasrara).** Located at the top of your head, the crown chakra will not open until all six of the other major chakras are balanced. When it is open, you experience the highest connection to the Universal Mind by your mental, physical, and spiritual self. The crown chakra controls the pineal gland.

The Universal Life Force enters the body through the crown chakra at the top of the head. As it works its way down through your body, it flows through the other centers. Once it spreads to the base chakra, it arouses the kundalini energy, which yogis believe sleeps in a coiled serpentine form.

It is the external Universal Life Force, which this book identi-
fies as the Universal Mind, which you first connect with when
you focus beyond your third eye to the top of your head. The
Universal Life Force energy is what you feel when your third
eye vibrates or swells. It is this external energy form that helps
increase psychic ability.

FINDING BALANCE

It is possible that one or more of your chakras may be blocked as a
result of many different situations. The cause may be stress, or it could
be a mental, spiritual, or physical condition. Be aware that it is almost
impossible to keep all of your chakras in balance all the time.

Once you grow sensitive to feeling the balance of your chakras,
you will be able to sense when the balance is broken. At that point,
you can take the steps to bring yourself back in balance.

The goal of this basic balance exercise is to open your crown
chakra at the top of your head to the unconditionally loving energy
of the Universe and let it flow downward through the third-eye
chakra and on to your other centers until it reaches your base
chakra. This will help you begin to balance the energy throughout your body. As you get comfortable with the circulation of the
Universal Flow, it may seem as if you are literally taking in this
positive energy with each deep breath.

Exercise: Open and Balance Your Chakras

Start by getting comfortable. Take a deep breath and exhale slowly.
Do this a couple more times, allowing yourself to relax more and
more with each breath. If any muscle is stiff, allow it to relax as you
continue to breathe slowly in and out. You may now close your eyes
and focus on your crown chakra at the top of your head. If for any

reason you feel overwhelmed by the energy or are suddenly flooded with psychic knowledge, you may always take a deep breath and open your eyes and return safely to your normal conscious world.

> If your crown chakra is opened and not balanced, the flow of energy may be overwhelming. This is particularly true when you open yourself to psychic energy. It can pulse through you and totally overcome you without warning. Knowing how to shut down the flow is as important as knowing how to open it.

Allow yourself to feel the Universal Energy as it streams at a comfortable rate through your crown and down into your third eye. You may feel the warmth of unconditional love and peace as it flows from the Universe. For a few brief moments, allow yourself to absorb this peaceful and loving feeling as each breath brings it more and more into focus.

Feel the Energy Flow Downward

You may allow yourself to focus on this loving and peaceful energy as it moves downward to your throat chakra. As the energy reaches this center, you may feel the Universal vibration first relax and then open that area of your body. You may feel the love and peace flowing from your crown to your third eye to your throat with every deep breath you take. Take a few moments to enjoy this blend of energy as it resonates with each breath, in through your crown chakra to your third-eye chakra and out through your throat chakra.

Now allow the Universal Energy to flow downward until you focus on your heart chakra. Feel the peaceful and loving energy as it brings the warmth of the unconditionally loving energy of the Universe to your heart. Feel the vibrations as they tune this important center around your heart. You may feel the loving and peaceful energy with each deep breath as it flows in through your crown to your third eye, down to your throat, and out through your heart chakra. Take a few moments and enjoy the love and peace as it spreads through and balances these chakras.

Next you may feel the peace and love of the Universal Energy as you focus it downward to your solar-plexus chakra. Feel the positive vibrations of your solar-plexus center balancing itself as you breathe the Universal Energy in (through your crown to your third eye to your throat and heart chakras) and out (through your solar-plexus chakra). With each deep breath you take, you may feel the unconditionally loving energy of the Universe flowing downward. Take a few moments and enjoy the special sensations created by the balancing of these energy centers.

Experience the Kundalini Energy

Now, when you are ready, allow yourself to focus the peace and love of your Universal Energy Flow down to your sacral chakra. As you feel the golden-light vibrations bring balance to this center, you may be aware of the kundalini energy that waits below, coiled and ready to combine its strength and power with the Universal Flow. With each deep breath, you may feel the peace and love of the Universe as it flows down through your third-eye chakra, to your throat, heart, and solar plexus, and out through your sacral chakra. Take a few moments to enjoy the peace and love of the Universe as it flows downward through your centers.

Your spine is the main conduit for the Universal Energy Flow. As you breathe in, focus on the love and peace that is entering through your crown. As you breathe out, feel the love and peace flowing through the energy center that you have focused on.

Now you may allow yourself to focus the Universal Flow downward all the way to your root chakra. Feel the power of the kundalini energy as it combines with the Universal Energy and lifts it upward. As you breathe downward, the unconditionally loving energy flows through your crown to your third eye, to your throat, heart, solar plexus, and navel, and out through your root chakra, as you feel peace and love. Exhale and feel the vast power of the Universe as it pulsates throughout your entire body. As your chakras vibrate in total harmony, they now open your crown chakra to the divine wisdom of the Universe.

Receive Your Knowledge

Spend some time in this peaceful and loving state as you experience the divine energy of unconditional Universal Love flowing throughout your body. Your head may naturally feel as if it is lifting upward so your crown chakra can experience a direct connection to the Universal Energy Flow. You may slowly allow your arms to open and float up from your body. Your hands may open with their palms cupping slightly and facing upward to further receive the peace and love of the Universe.

Imagine that you are also drawing loving energy up from the earth to create a perfect balance with the vast heavens above. You are now completely immersed in the unconditional flow of loving Universal Energy. You may feel the incredible power of the Universe as it combines with your internal and external guidance systems and your Belief. At this time, you are totally open to the peace and love of the Divine. In this state, your intuitive gifts are now in balance and harmony. You are ready to receive the appropriate knowledge provided by the Universe for your psychic development.

Count Back Up

When you are ready to come back to your conscious mind, you may count slowly from zero to five. As you continue to breathe slowly and deeply, you may bring your feeling of peace and love back to your conscious state. When you get to five, take a deep breath, open your eyes, and continue to feel the positive flow of the Universe through your balanced chakra centers. You may feel grounded in the divine love of the Universe.

This exercise is very basic. If you want to incorporate your own techniques, you are encouraged to do so. Each of you will have a different experience as you work with your chakras.

MASSAGE BENEFITS BALANCING

If you would like to help your energy centers open, you may want to consider adding light massage techniques to your balancing exercise. As you focus on your crown chakra, you may gently massage the top of your head. Move the tips of the three longest fingers of one of your hands in a circular motion. After a few moments, let your hand return to its previous position as you focus on the peace and love that are balancing the crown chakra.

When you focus on the third-eye chakra, continue this same massage technique. Always keep your touch light as you move your hand slowly in a circular motion in the center of your forehead. You can work your way down through the rest of your chakra centers using this same technique. If for any reason you feel discomfort, discontinue the massage and either focus on your chakra exercise without it or open your eyes and come back to full consciousness, relaxed, calm, and filled with peace and love.

When a blocked energy center is opened suddenly, the rush of energy can trigger a spontaneous psychic image. This often is the case when you experience massage, Reiki, or another method of healing art for the first time.

Another method of massaging your energy centers is to work with your aura. Place the open palm of one of your hands approximately two inches above an energy center. Slowly begin to circle the palm of your hand in a counterclockwise motion. You may feel pressure, heat, a tickle, or a prickly feeling as your hand moves over the spot.

BALANCE THROUGH COLOR

Each of the seven energy chakras also has a specific color that is produced when the energy of that center is in balance. If you are visual, it may help you to balance your chakras by visualizing the proper color for each center. You may add the color imagery to your chakra-balancing exercise.

Here is a list of colors for each of the seven chakras:

* The base, or root, chakra is red.

* The sacral, or belly, chakra is orange.

* The solar-plexus chakra is yellow.

* The heart chakra is green.

* The throat chakra is blue.

* The third-eye, or forehead, chakra is a deep indigo.

* The crown chakra is a white or violet.

You may be able to feel energy in relationship to color. You can focus on red and go right to your root chakra and feel the base of your kundalini energy. Or you can focus on the color green and project it to your heart chakra.

As you begin to practice getting in tune with your energy centers, you may want to practice opening and balancing them in a natural progression from your third eye downward and finally back to the crown again. The more you understand the vibrational level of each center, the more it can help you in your psychic development.

Exercise: Find Balance Using Your Senses

This exercise will help you use your five senses to open and balance your seven chakras. First, focus on your breathing. As you breathe slowly in and out, let your body relax. When you are ready, allow yourself to begin to focus on your crown-chakra energy center. Focus on a pure, white, loving energy as you inhale. Let this beautiful white energy flow over any negative colors and sweep them out of your crown chakra as you exhale. You may feel a certain vibration that is special to that center. You may be able to sense a certain tone that helps to open and balance your crown chakra.

As you breathe in and out, you may sense that perhaps there is a special smell or even a taste that you can relate to your crown-chakra energy center. Experiment using your different senses to help you open and balance your crown chakra and bring the strongest image into a clear focus. Now anchor that image with a touch to your crown or with a special word or phrase. Release your connection, and practice reconnecting to your crown chakra by triggering your anchor.

When you are ready, you may focus on your third-eye chakra. Use the same technique that you developed for opening and balancing your crown chakra. Engage as many of your five different senses as you are comfortable with: sight (color), sound, feeling, taste, or smell.

Once you have achieved a clear focus on your third-eye center, create an anchor for it. Now practice disengaging and reconnecting again. When you are comfortable with opening and balancing your third-eye chakra, move downward to your heart chakra. Follow the same process until you have opened and balanced all of your chakras.

Let all seven chakras balance together in a blend of color and energy. You may use cues, imagery, and remembered sensations from all five of your senses to experience this Universal Flow. Let your physical, mental, and spiritual bodies feel unified in total harmony with the Universe.

DEVELOP YOUR ABILITIES THROUGH YOUR CHAKRAS

You may already have had a psychic experience through one of your different chakra centers when you unwittingly opened up to the Universal Flow. When it happened, you might not have been aware of what took place. This explanation may help you get a better perspective on what may take place when you have a psychic experience through one or more of your chakras.

The lower chakras are considered to be more primitive in the range of psychic abilities. It is the root, sacral, and solar-plexus energy centers that you open to be a medium or to communicate with the dead. You may also use these chakras when you experience psychic dreams. The lower chakra levels are considered to be more spontaneous than controlled.

The heart chakra is where you intuitively feel. If you are working with massage or other healing techniques and open your heart chakra, you may be flooded with the other person's physical, mental, or spiritual negative feelings. If you aren't prepared for the energy flow, you may find yourself internalizing it. Without an outlet, this energy will overrun yours, and it may affect your balance and even your health. If, on the other hand, you have some awareness of what might happen, you can let the energy flow through your heart chakra. Channeled this way, it has a great potential for healing those who receive the positive energy of peace and love.

The ability to see through extrasensory perception is called clairvoyance. When your third-eye chakra is open, you may be able to see on nonphysical planes. You may see as well as hear your guides or angels. You may also be able to see the past or future.

When your throat chakra is open, you may have the ability to hear your guides or angels. You may receive verbal advice or even warnings about yourself or others. As you identify and learn to rely on the communication that comes to you through your guides, you will learn to trust their accuracy.

When the crown chakra is open, you may be able to travel to and experience different planes. You may find yourself floating out of your body and experiencing the vast power of the Universal Flow.

Work with Your Chakras

Now you may go back to your chakra exercises and begin to identify your psychic gifts. First, let yourself come into balance with all your energy centers. It is always good to center yourself when starting a psychic exercise. Do this by connecting to your Belief and your internal and external guidance systems. Feel the peace and unconditional love of the Universe and believe that any intuitive image is given to you for a special purpose.

Once you have done this, start with your lower chakras and open up to connections from the Other Side. You may feel the power of the kundalini as it combines with the Universal Flow. You may open to spontaneous psychic intuition that is given to you by the unconditionally loving energy of the Universe.

When you are ready, open your heart chakra to healing energies and positive feelings. Next open your throat chakra to the communication of your guides and angels. Look for the clear visions through your third eye, and finally, let yourself float to other planes of psychic experiences guided by the golden thread along the white beam of your crown chakra. When you are ready, slowly bring yourself back to consciousness, filled with the love and peace of the Universe and in tune with your psychic experience through your chakras.

Remember, the way you work through your energy centers is different from anyone else. You may experiment with all the material in this chapter and develop a technique that is best for you. As you work with your chakras, you may find yourself opening more and more to your psychic gifts.

CHAPTER 6

MEET AND IDENTIFY YOUR GUIDES

Does everything in your life happen by chance or fate, or is there some sort of a force that exists around you to help you through life? It is an age-old question but one that continues to baffle. As you continue on the path of developing your psychic abilities, you will discover, if you haven't already, that you are not traveling alone. You will notice that there are just too many synchronicities happening to deny that something else may very well be involved in the direction of your journey and who or what you encounter along the way. Whatever these forces may be—Edgar Cayce called them "the invisible empire"—you can count on them to guide you along your life map and protect you from harm. This chapter will give you the opportunity to meet and identify your team of spiritual advisers.

YOUR SPIRITUAL COMPANIONS

There are many terms to describe the spirit forces that exist beyond our current accepted reality. Spirits, guides, angels, power animals, and gatekeepers are just a few of the names that have been used by those who experience a connection to the unknown world around them.

The guides and other spirits that are described in this book are there for good. If you feel that you are getting negative advice or communication, you should stop contact with them and seek a qualified counselor in your area.

There are many books that tell you how to meet and connect to your guides or angels. The premise of this book is that you are already connected, even though you may not realize it yet. It is the goal of the exercises in this chapter for you to become more aware of the unknown forces that are already with you, and that you will begin to develop a way to communicate with them as you learn to trust in the information you are receiving.

Do you believe that you have an unseen helper around you? Are you already aware of this force? And if not, do you trust that you will come to learn more about it? Regardless of what you believe, if you focus on good and positive feelings, you may be amazed at the incredible results.

Be Aware of Your Life's Miracles

Do you believe that there are miracles that happen in your life? If so, when and how often do they take place? Are your miracles generally large events that happen periodically, or are they part of your everyday existence? Do you know who works these wondrous acts? Is it God, an angel, a deceased relative or friend, a spirit guide, or something or someone else?

> A miracle is something that happens beyond the scope of reality. Miracles are usually attributed to a supernatural power that intervenes in the normal course of events and changes their expected or predictable outcome. Examples include miraculous healings and changes in negative weather patterns that forecasters had failed to identify.

Miracles come in all forms. There are big events that are just too unbelievable to dismiss as nonmiracles; these are the events that force us to admit results sometimes happen that are beyond the abilities of humans to achieve. Big miracles are often life-changing events, such as an unexpected financial windfall when it was desperately needed, or a positive improvement in health against all medical odds. There seem to be no logical explanations for these outcomes. Little miracles are often day-to-day events, such as synchronicities of being in the right place at the right time, or coincidences, such as accidentally crossing paths with someone you needed or wanted to see. These events are often overlooked because they happen so naturally that you begin to take them for granted. Do you keep a record of the miracles that you recognize? Here are some suggestions that may help you keep track:

* Pick a time each day to be aware of miracles.

* Start by thanking your Source or Belief for already taking care of your request.

* Keep a record of what you ask of your Source or Belief.

* Review the day to see if you received any miracles you asked for.

* Review the day to see what miracles, large or small, took place that you didn't ask for.

* Be aware of what you received; sometimes a miracle is granted in a different way than you requested.

* Acknowledge a resistance as something that might be leading to a miracle.

* Give thanks to your Source for all miracles large and small, known and unknown.

The more you become aware of the events in your life that take place without a logical explanation, the more you will begin to see the miracles that have been around you all along. Keeping a record of daily events will help you get in tune with your guides.

Be Careful of What You Ask For

If you focus on wanting something, you may get what you wanted, but it might not be what you really needed. If you get what you need, you might not realize it because you are so focused on what you wanted.

Let's say, for example, that you need a new car. You ask for and expect to receive a new car. You might even try to manifest it. Then, you receive an opportunity to get a used car; it isn't new, but it's just right for what you need. If you are still focused on the new car, you will not appreciate the miracle of getting the car you needed.

When you request assistance, carefully consider the words that you use in asking for the right solution for all concerned at the time of the request. Believe, in the case of our new-car example, in the gift of the right vehicle that will help you with your life work. Consider requesting with gratitude for the right words to come out of your mouth and the right thoughts to come through your mind. In the same manner, when developing your psychic abilities, request that the right information come at the right time, with the intention that you might use this information in the best way for the greater good.

Acknowledge Resistance

When things aren't going exactly the way you had planned, a miracle might be working behind the scenes. It is very easy to focus so strongly on what you think should happen that you miss the reason why your Source is taking the actions that it is. Be open to what is best for the whole in the long run.

If you pay attention and work with the resistances in your life, rather than fighting them, you will become aware of the miracle that may be behind any resistances you encounter. If you force your way through a resistance instead of accepting it, you may find yourself where you really don't want to be.

ANGELIC GUIDES

The word "angel" comes from the Greek, and it means "messenger." Angels are usually depicted as human-like beings in long, flowing robes with halos over their heads and a pair of wings to help them travel between heaven and earth. In early Christian times, angels were called demons and could be either good or bad. Later, the term was expanded to refer to the evil angels who are disciples of Lucifer. This book is about connecting to positive angels who are here to help you help others and yourself.

Rudolf Steiner, a philosopher and spiritualist, believed that there exists an ascending order of spirits that includes Angels, Archangels, Archai, Exusiai, Dynameis, Kyriotetes, Thrones, Cherubim, and Seraphim. Each level has more responsibility in the role that they play with the human race. Angels are close to our level of consciousness and are therefore the most recognizable form of spirit messenger. Steiner claimed that he was shown this system of order through psychic visions.

In Christian tradition, there are seven archangels: Gabriel, Raphael, Michael, Uriel, Jophiel, Zadkiel, and Samuel. Lucifer was the eighth archangel. He was cast out of heaven and became the leader of the dark angels, or demons.

It is possible that humankind was much more open to the spirit world before religious movements, such as early Christianity, tried to eliminate views that were not part of their doctrine. Many early pagan beliefs were absorbed by the more organized religions, and these early beliefs then changed as time went by. As an example, early pagan celebration dates were adapted to Christian celebrations, including Christmas and Easter. It was in this manner that the good demons (daimons) of the Greeks became the evil demons of the Bible. At the same time, the Christian religion embraced the concept of angels as the good messengers of God.

You could theorize that early paintings, which influence our view of what an angel looks like, came from an actual encounter with a spirit by the artist. The halo or golden glow may first have been seen as an aura. The energy about a spirit could very well shimmer, creating that effect. Because the spirit may have been seen suspended above the ground, wings may have been added to make a more realistic picture. It is possible for a spirit or angel to appear to each of you in a manner that is acceptable to you. Your angels or spirits may or may not look like anything that is described in this book.

Guardian Angels

A guardian is defined as someone who takes charge or care of someone else. A guardian angel is considered to be a spirit being that watches over a human.

Do you consider yourself to have a guardian angel or angels to watch over you? Have you ever seen your angels? If so, what do they look like? Can you hear your angels speaking to you? If so, what are they saying? How often and under what circumstances do your angels visit you—daily, weekly, or only occasionally?

Can you feel your angels around you? If so, when do you feel them? Have your angels produced certain smells or tastes for you to experience? Have you ever heard their wings or other sounds that let you know they are with you?

You do not need to see an angel to recognize that one is there with you. Validation can happen in many ways. Keeping a record of your miracles also reminds you that your team of angels is at work, whether you see them or not. If you feel that you have angels watching over you, then give them credit for the good job they are doing.

GUIDES FROM THE OTHER SIDE

Your guides may be people you already know. It is possible that a friend or relative who is now on the Other Side could act as a guide for you in this lifetime and is looking out for you. Have you been paying attention to the clues that might tell you whether you have such a guide? If you haven't, that's not uncommon—most people don't keep track of the guides who are helping out in their lives.

Do you have a feeling that there is someone who has passed over who still keeps watch over you on this side? If so, who could it be? Perhaps you know or suspect you know who is there, but you can't see for yourself. You may get validation from almost anywhere. It could be a sudden reminder of something special when the person was alive.

Once you accept that there is a good possibility of a guide or guides connected to you, you can begin to develop confidence that there really is someone there to help you handle both minor and major problems. You can actually have a conversation with your guides, even though it seems to be a one-way conversation. Just believing that someone hears you can give you confidence that you are not alone.

If you are having trouble defining who is watching over you from the Other Side, you may want to go for a psychic reading. A competent and ethical psychic may have the ability to recognize who is watching out for and working with you.

The Other Side may not appear to you while you are in a waking state. Many times your guides will visit you in your dream state. This is especially true if you have an active conscious mind that is constantly cluttered with your thoughts. Your psychic communication often comes into your awareness when your active mind stops to rest. The only time you relax may be when you sleep.

SPIRIT GUIDES

In addition to angels and the souls of those who have passed on to the Other Side, there are other nonphysical entities that exist in the spirit world. A spirit may be a fairy, ghost, power animal, or another entity. Some people believe that spirits are evil and fear that communication with a spirit is working with the devil. Others are afraid that communicating with spirits will lead to losing control of their body, mind, and spirit.

The fear of spirit possession is very real to many people. It is possible that some people who are not grounded in a strong faith can leave themselves vulnerable to encounters with negative energy. Making sure to surround yourself with your protective bubble of unconditionally loving energy can help you on your journey of psychic development. At the same time, if you encounter a strong negative force for any reason, stop what you are doing and seek the advice of a professional psychologist or clergy member who has a background in working with spirit possession.

An exorcism is a rite that is performed by a priest of the Catholic Church to rid a victim of the evil spirit or spirits that possess him. Other religions perform their own type of exorcisms. For example, Pentecostal Christians use the laying-on of hands.

On the other hand, you may consider a spirit to be something that can be your guide and help you through life. You may have an image in your mind of what a spirit looks like. You may already be working with your spirit. A spirit who is there to help you is called a spirit guide.

You may consider your positive spirit guides as part of a team that is there to help you on your journey through life. Take a moment to think back over your life, and you may find that there were times when you had a spirit guide with you. The following questions are designed to help you remember clues that you may have dismissed in the past.

Who's Been Guiding You?

For a brief moment, take a relaxing breath, exhale, and think back to your childhood. When you were very little, did you live in an environment where you played and talked with spirits? If so, how old were you when you first met them, and how old were you when you stopped communicating with them?

How did you experience these childhood encounters? Did you see, hear, feel, smell, or get a taste of whom or what they were? Did you ever tell anyone about them? If so, what was their response? Did they believe you and encourage you to continue or tell you to stop fantasizing?

If you have had a form of spirit being with you, is the being still there? If so, how do you communicate with it? With which of the five senses do you experience it? If you don't, when was the last time you were aware of it? If it is not there now, can you imagine what it was like when it was with you? Was there more than one spirit with you?

The spirits you may have communicated with could have had particular shapes and roles, such as any of the following:

✳ **Fairies:** These are spirits that resemble tiny people. Fairies live in the woods and are known for their magical powers. They are a part of Celtic lore and are especially popular with children, probably due to their small size. A fairyland is a magical place where children live in a fantasy world full of enchanting wonderment.

* **Gatekeepers:** In the psychic world, these are spirit guards who watch out for you as you travel about in other realms. A gatekeeper is your strong and powerful guide and protector. You can count on this being to help keep your energy centers in balance as he or she controls what enters and leaves.

* **Power animals:** Animals have been connected to mysticism since time immemorial. If you have a power animal, it could be one from nature, such as a wolf or a bear. It could be a domestic pet, perhaps one that crossed over but still lingers with you to watch over and comfort you.

Whatever your spirits are, they may visit you in your dreams. Do you have dreams that include forms of spirit guides or animals? If so, how often do you dream about them? Do they come for specific reasons that relate to your life situation at that time? Do they have messages for you from beyond?

MEET YOUR GUIDES

Let's take some time and begin to meet your spiritual guides. Remember, each of you has a different relationship and connection with them. You may or may not see them, feel them, hear them, smell them, or otherwise sense them. On the other hand, you may get a clear view and understanding of who they are and why they are with you. If you're ready, find a relaxing place and get comfortable.

Exercise: Contact Your Guides

Take a deep breath, exhale, close your eyes, and begin to feel the connection through your crown chakra down to your third-eye chakra. Allow yourself to feel the loving and peaceful energy of the Universe as it flows downward into your body. Feel the unconditionally loving energy of the Universe around your total being as it forms a protective bubble. Feel the positive energy that keeps you in balance and leaves you free to be open to the Universe's guides that have been assigned to you. Let yourself enjoy a brief moment of total freedom filled with peace and love.

Remember, you can always bring yourself out of an altered state of focus. All you have to do is take a deep breath, exhale, open your eyes, and come back to your conscious mind, feeling positive and safe.

Ask your Belief permission to meet one or more of your guides in any positive form they may take. Allow yourself to relax, breathe in and out, and wait for a feeling of affirmation. This affirmation may come as a direct image, a voice, a pleasant sound, a feeling, or even a smell. You may experience nothing at first, so just wait patiently and believe that the right images will come to you. It is possible that this is not the right time to meet your guides.

You may get a faint image, or a lot of images swirling together. You may see colors, or you may hear a whole group of voices. If everything is going too fast, ask your Belief for help in slowing down your images. If you can, focus on just one image and concentrate on defining to yourself what you are sensing. Allow your guides to become comfortable in revealing themselves to you.

Many people have an expectation of what they think their guides should be. You may or may not get the images you expected. Just being in the flow of positive peace and love is good for you. Just imagining your guides will bring you closer to them.

Make the Connection

If you are able to sense your guides, can you communicate with them? If so, which sense do you feel most comfortable using? Even if you see nothing, you may still ask questions. You may receive your answers in pictures, by voice or other sounds, by feelings that you can translate into words, or through positive and negative tastes and smells. You may have feelings in certain places in your body or some other sensation or image. You may ask if there is a name that you can call your guide(s).

The first step is to get an understanding of what you may be telling yourself through your guides. You may ask for guidance in many different aspects of your life, from health to your soul's purpose. Don't expect an answer right away. It might come then, or it might come in the near future. Always keep the feeling of Universal peace and love flowing through you when you are making the connection to your guides. It is possible that you may know that they are there but that you may never really see them. That's okay, for the important thing is that they are with you.

CHANNELING SPIRITS

Another form of psychic communication and guidance is channeling. A channel is a conduit for something to pass through. A psychic channel is a person who has another entity or spirit communicate through him or her. This may be a voluntary or involuntary action on the part of the host body—the channel isn't always aware of what is taking place. Channeling can happen when you are in a trance or asleep.

When you act as a channel, your voice and mannerisms may change to reflect the personality of the entity that is coming through. During this time, the spirit may convey information through speech, automatic writing, or even different artistic forms. Many channels bring a message of peace from a higher source of knowledge.

Experiencing Channeling

If you'd like to try your hand at channeling, it's a good idea to begin with someone experienced with the concept, like a hypnotherapist. She can help facilitate you into a deep altered state of focus in a safe and positive environment.

You can also try automatic writing or typing by allowing yourself to enter a relaxed trance state, leaving your fingers free to be used by the spirit. Just ask your Belief that the right messages for that moment come through your hands and fingers. Like all other forms of psychic development, practice and patience will help your technique to improve.

It is possible to channel when you are fully awake. Ask your Belief to let the right words come through your mouth. Believing that this will happen will actually help you to channel Universal truths that are good for both you and the people you are speaking with.

THE AKASHIC BOOK OF RECORDS

Another source of information relating to your soul's development is the Akashic Book of Records. The word "Akashic" comes from Hindu Sanskrit and means a place or space in the Universe that is all encompassing. Within this realm is housed all the knowledge of the Universe. It is believed that every detail of every soul's existence is recorded there. This is where Edgar Cayce traveled for information on the past lives of the individual for whom he was doing a reading.

Exercise: Visit the Akashic Book of Records

To visit the Akashic Book of Records, get comfortable, take a deep breath, exhale, and relax. You may focus on your third eye and bring your whole body into tune and balance. Feel the positive energy of peace and unconditional love filling your body and the Universe's protective bubble surrounding you.

When you are ready, allow yourself to float upward until you come to the great Hall of Records, knowing that you can always open your eyes and return to full consciousness feeling safe and secure. You may ask that you be able to see and read the sections on your soul that would be most helpful to you at this moment. If permission is granted, let yourself be guided to the proper place in the records and experience the information with all five senses. You may want to follow a specific theme through several of your past lives, or you may want to focus on one life.

When checking into a past life, always look to see who in that life might also be in your current life. Compare the roles you each have had, and look for unresolved karma. Also ask to understand the theme of that lifetime so that you may apply the knowledge to help you improve in this lifetime. When you're ready, bring yourself back to earth and back to full consciousness, totally aware of your surroundings.

HONE YOUR PSYCHIC SIGHT

One of the most common psychic abilities is clairvoyance, or psychic sight. In this chapter, you will have the opportunity to examine different types of clairvoyance and explore your own visual gifts. However, it is important to realize that while many people see in their minds, this may not be true for you. If you are not a visual person, this may not be the gift you possess—remember that vision is only one of five senses, and all of your senses provide you with your psychic information.

VISUAL IMAGES

Most of you experience visual images in your conscious mind as well as in your unconscious and your Universal Mind. Your conscious visual images are experienced live—what you are seeing is happening at that moment. Conscious sight is the reality, as it is shared with other people. When you see a picture with your eyes, it is then stored in your unconscious memory.

Most people have unconscious minds that are capable of replaying the stored, conscious visual images at a later time. Your unconscious mind will replay these pictures in the way that your conscious mind processed them. Five people might all share the exact same experience and then recall it, through their unconscious minds, differently. Each one may get part of the experience correct and part of it wrong. Each person is replaying what he recalled from the experience when it actually happened.

Second Sight

In addition to your conscious, external visual reality experiences, you may also have the gift of clairvoyance, or second sight. You may already be aware of and using this gift. Or you may have had negative psychic images in the past and have chosen to ignore or block them. Second sight may appear to you at any time, usually when you are least expecting it.

Second sight can combine with your other senses and may be experienced in all three phases of time—past, present, and future. The past images may come from your present lifetime or from a time period back in history. They may relate to your life, or they may have nothing to do with it.

Second sight into the future means seeing something that has not yet happened. These images may just "pop" into your head and may not be connected to your own future. If your third-eye chakra is open and unbalanced, you may receive second-sight images relating to any place in the world. It is always important to remember to keep yourself grounded and surrounded by the Universe's protective bubble of loving energy.

Realistic and Symbolic Visual Images

There are two different ways that you may experience clairvoyance. The most common way is to see a realistic visual image. It can come to you either when you are awake or when you are asleep and may relate to the past or the future. It can also be triggered by what you are experiencing at a particular moment in time.

Clairvoyance literally means "clear seeing." A psychic who is clairvoyant has the ability to see what is generally acknowledged to be unseen or not real. A psychic who understands her power of clairvoyance accepts it as part of her reality.

The other form of second sight is symbolic. Symbolic imagery often involves the kinesthetic sense. The images may provide you with a "gut feeling" of their meaning. All psychics must learn to develop their own interpretations of the symbols they visualize.

TYPES OF CLAIRVOYANCE

There are several different types of clairvoyance, including the ability to see through objects, over long distances, into the past (an ability known as retrocognition or postcognition), or into the future (known as precognition). Clairvoyance may involve being able to see health conditions of people and/or animals, having psychic dreams, visualizing other worlds and beings, and seeing divine images.

You may be able to have psychic experiences in all of the different forms of visual images, or in some, or in none. Understanding your natural mental image strengths will help you to recognize your clairvoyant abilities. Don't worry if you are not clairvoyant. It is just one way of being psychic.

Many people with the gift of second sight can see into the future or the past, whether through dreaming or through contact with spirits, angels, or guides. The more you become aware of and understand what you are already seeing in your mind's eye, the more confidence you will have in trusting and using your psychic gifts in the future.

Mental telepathy is mind-to-mind communication and is part of your range of psychic abilities. Visual telepathy is the communication of a visual image from one person to another. It is different from second sight or clairvoyance because only your mind is involved.

Seeing Spiritual Beings

One aspect of clairvoyance is seeing spiritual beings like angels or spirit guides. Note that this isn't the same as seeing ghosts, who contact you on a physical plane. A spirit usually contacts you from your inner mind—either your unconscious or your Universal Mind—and is seen through your mind's eye. You may have the ability to see the spiritual beings that exist around other people. If that is the case, you could help others know what they do not see in themselves.

Learn from your dreams—they may be of symbolic nature, especially if they involve a specific animal or other spirits. If you can see spirits in your dreams, you have an even greater opportunity to develop an understanding of how they are here to work with you.

Spirit guides can help you navigate successfully through your life map. They have the ability to communicate with your Universal Mind and to gather wisdom that will help you make positive decisions. Although they most often appear in human form, they may be experienced in other shapes as well.

Power Animals

Spiritual communication may come in the form of a power animal that is there to guide and protect you. If you feel that you have a power animal, it can be a strong element in guiding you through life. Just the image of strength that goes with a power animal can give you courage to take positive risks. These risks can be incorporated into your Belief System, and it becomes easier to overcome the fear of failure. If you believe that something, including a power animal, goes with you to guide you, you will be more open to being in tune with your life map.

Angelic Communication

Your spirit guide may take on the form of an angel. You may have more than one angelic being guiding you. These guides may appear as people you recognize who have passed over to the Other Side, or they may take on shapes of those you have never met. They may visit you on a regular basis or only at times when you need a little help. If you can see your angels, you have been given a special gift from your psychic side. They may help provide you with clairvoyant images for other people.

PICTURES OF THE FUTURE AND PAST

Precognition is a more direct form of psychic ability because it can allow you to see an event as it will happen in the future, rather than having a spirit guide who will share information about future events. Most often, precognition works as a realistic image, but it can also be viewed in symbolic form. The event can be recognizable and related to you or someone you know, or it can be something that you know nothing about. You may see it only once, or it can occur over and over. It can come to you in a dream or a vision.

Scrying is a form of divination that uses certain visual aids (like crystal balls, tea leaves, clouds, mirrors, or even the swirl of cream in coffee) to help produce the proper visual trance for seeing into the future. When you look at these objects, your eyes will go out of focus, and you will engage your second sight.

The earliest psychic images a young person may receive are often precognitions. They appear out of nowhere, and, more often than not, they predict an event that is related to an impending tragedy—the death of a loved one or an accident. A young person who has seen signs of a future event may feel responsible for it when it occurs.

Looking Back at the Past

The opposite of precognition is postcognition or retrocognition—seeing into the past to events that have already occurred. The images could be related to the individual's own lifetime, but not necessarily. The event seen could even be from a distant lifetime or time period. A location or an object may help induce a postcognition trance.

One form of postcognition is time-bending. There are those who believe that they can merge different time periods for the purpose of healing the past. They project themselves back into events from the past so that they may release the negative aura that may have been trapped in that time period. It is believed that if humankind can heal history by resolving the mistakes of the past, the future will not be caught in the same unresolved karma.

LET YOUR IMAGINATION FLOW

Have you ever experienced any of the visual images discussed so far and dismissed them as just your imagination? If so, you are not alone. Many people never give their psychic ability of second sight a chance to help guide them through life. In fact, those of you who are very creative and see a lot of images in your head may overlook psychic images as just "imagination." But was that really all it was?

If you have a good visual imagination, you might consider letting yourself go on an imaginary adventure. You don't have to worry about what you imagine just yet—it doesn't necessarily have to be psychic information. If you encounter negative images that cause you to worry, take a moment and thank your Belief or spiritual guide for helping you bring about positive outcomes, and if for any reason you begin to feel uncomfortable, you may always discontinue the session by taking a deep breath and returning to full consciousness.

As you let your imagination run wild, make note of your thoughts and compare them to events in your life and the real world. These notes may record events that have already happened—that is, from the past—but you should also note events that happen in accordance with the way you envisioned them. It is okay for you not to fully understand the process that is taking place as you imagine. All you really need to understand is that imagination is an ability that you have. Just accept it and allow yourself to take a very large step in your psychic development. The more you work with it, the more you will learn to trust your psychic gift of second sight.

When you let your imagination flow, always make sure you are grounded. By connecting yourself to your Belief and your bubble of loving Universal Energy, you are taking steps to protect yourself from any negative images that you may experience.

Focusing

The unseen is with you all the time, as it is with everyone. It's just that no one sees it exactly the same way. It takes time and patience to learn to trust that what you see is a reality on a different plane. Once you have learned to trust, even though you may not be able to explain it to someone else's satisfaction, you will be able to rely on your psychic clairvoyant gift.

Believe it or not, to use your psychic gift, it is best to let your mind and vision drift out of focus. Have you ever stared at a multi-image hologram, a picture that has at least two different images? It is hard to see the second image until you relax your stare. In other words, to be in focus, you need to be out of focus.

It is possible to become so focused on the psychic image that you forget how to refocus on your reality image. If you feel this happening to you, take a deep breath, exhale, and release your focus on the psychic image.

Your psychic image may begin as a vague picture that superimposes itself over your reality image. If you are in a convenient location and situation, you may find that closing your eyes and focusing on your third eye will help you to sharpen your psychic image. Remember to keep yourself grounded in your Belief and let yourself be protected by your bubble of Universal loving energy.

Discerning Auras

As you have already learned, an aura is an energy field that surrounds all living things as well as places, events, and objects. Although the feeling of the aura is important, so is its visual form. Auras may be seen in colors or simply in wavy colorless lines. If you can see auras, you have been given an opportunity to gain a wealth of knowledge about many different situations and conditions that others may not have access to.

It is also possible for some of you to see the auras of objects. You may be able to see negative or positive energies coming from particular places or personal belongings. If you can see this type of aura, you are sensing the energies of people who have left an energy impression. The aura may be created by the energy of people who are there at that moment, or perhaps it is leftover residue from a previous time. It is very possible to see the auras from negative events that happened hundreds of years ago.

PSYCHIC-SIGHT PRACTICE

Psychic visual experiences differ from person to person. Your particular visions may come from either inside yourself from your mind's eye, or from an external source. The goal here is to encourage you to identify, develop, and work with your clairvoyant psychic abilities. And the first step is to identify how you see.

You may discover that you have ability at second sight that is different from the abilities addressed in this chapter. Your mind is special and unique. It does have psychic abilities, but they may or may not be visual. If you do have the gift of clairvoyance, it is likely connected to one or more of your other four senses.

The following exercises will help you identify and begin working with your visual psychic abilities. Although you can do these exercises on your own, it can be both fun and educational to do them in a group. When you compare your second sight to that of others, you may be amazed at how different or similar they are.

When you begin to practice psychic development exercises, it is very important for you to be in tune with your physical, mental, and spiritual self. This includes being spiritually grounded and in the proper frame of mind, as well as having a full stomach.

Exercise: Images Under Your Eyelids

You may begin this exercise by finding a place that is comfortable and relaxing for you. You can either sit or lie down. When you're ready, take a deep breath, exhale slowly, and let your eyes go out of focus as you concentrate for a moment on your crown chakra and feel the positive, loving energy of the Universe as it flows down to your third-eye chakra. You may take a few moments and experience the rest of your energy centers coming into balance. As you continue to breathe slowly in and out, you may feel the loving and peaceful energy of the Universe entering your body. You may feel the protective bubble of the Universe surrounding you as you examine your psychic gifts of second sight.

When you are comfortable and ready, focus your mind's eye on the images that are behind your eyelids. You may see an image clearly, or it may be out of focus. It is possible that the images you see are moving so fast that it is hard to focus on any one of them. If that is the case, allow yourself to relax even more and begin to slow down the speed of your images. This may be hard to do at first, but as you continue to practice, you should be able to bring your images into sync with your focus.

If you are able to see images under your eyelids, what are they? How do they compare to the different types of second sight that were discussed earlier in this chapter? Are they similar or different? Are your images comfortable or uncomfortable? If an image is uncomfortable, can you change it to another image?

Can you interpret your images to understand their meanings? You might ask your Universal Mind to help provide you with answers to any questions you may have. The answer may not come right away. Be patient, and remain alert to your insights. The answers may come from within or without.

Can you get images about the past or the future? Can you see your guides, or angels? Do you have images that relate to health or to your higher power? Are there any other images that you can see under your eyelids, and can their meanings be understood? When you are ready, take a deep breath, exhale, and return to consciousness in a positive, relaxed mood.

You may not have any images at all, and if so, that's okay. Clairvoyance may not be your psychic strength. It is possible that you can see colors behind your eyelids. It might be one color, or different colors that appear in various shapes or forms.

Exercise: Dream Imagery

Another exercise is to explore your dreams. As you relax and concentrate on your third eye, think about the dreams you've recently had. Do you dream in pictures? If so, are your dreams symbolic, realistic, or both? Do you travel to and explore places in your dreams? Do you dream of past lives or future events? Do you see in your dreams guides, angels, or loved ones who have passed over?

Another great way to work with your psychic intuition is simply to close your eyes and imagine. You might imagine a story with a theme that relates to your current life or from any point in time. Through this exercise, you may find insights into your life. Imagination is often a great method for finding the truth.

Exercise: See the Second Image

Have you ever had a second-sight experience when your eyes were wide open? If so, it may seem natural to you. If you rarely experience it—or if you never have—here is an exercise to try. Allow yourself to enter a relaxed state as you focus for a moment on your breathing.

Focus on your third-eye chakra. Your eyes will go slightly out of focus. You may suggest to yourself that you are comfortable and open to the psychic images that are waiting to help you grow in your intuitive development. Let your mind drift as you enjoy your connection to your visual energy center.

You may begin to be aware of a second image in your visual screen. Wait patiently and let this image slowly become clearer and clearer as it comes into focus. Let yourself see it clearly as you watch from the safety of your protective bubble of Universal Energy. Allow yourself to watch and process this image, and know that you can end it any time you want and return relaxed and positive to your conscious mind.

Keep a record of what you see and when you see it. Does your second sight relate to the past or the future? Are there times and places where it is easier to get these images? Can you look at a person and see energy or auras around her? Do the auras change?

Can you look into a person's body and see a medical problem? Can you create a healing image? Can you project your mind's eye to a remote location and see what is happening there at that very time?

CHAPTER 8

EXPLORE CLAIRAUDIENCE

Clairaudience literally means "clear hearing," and in psychic terms it is the ability to hear voices, sounds, or music that doesn't exist on the "normal" plane. These sounds may be internal, or may come to you from an outside source or even from a different time period or geographic location. Experiences of clairaudience may differ from individual to individual as much as those of second sight. Some people hear voices, while others are attuned to particular sounds or even music. In this chapter, you will learn how to identify and develop your psychic gift of clairaudience.

HEARING MORE

If you have the gift of clairaudience, you can hear more than most other people. Humans have been guided by their internal voices since the beginning of time. The Bible makes reference to the voice of God speaking to the prophets. The ancient Greeks received guidance from daimons, divine spirits offering wisdom usually heard in the mind through internal voices. The shamans of many cultures used the voices in their heads for divine advice.

Today, clairaudience is identified in many different forms. You may hear your own voice or one or more other voices. These voices may be heard as spirit guides, angels, deceased relatives or other spirits, symbolic figures, divine wisdom, or even animal guides. These voices may come when you are awake or dreaming.

> The voices in your head should offer you positive guidance and encouragement. If for any reason you hear constantly negative voices, you should immediately seek psychiatric or psychological professional help to understand what you are hearing.

You may only hear a voice from time to time when you have a specific need, or you may receive regular guidance from it—and there may be several different voices that you can perceive at different times. You may be able to project yourself out into the Universe and have a conference with brilliant minds on the Other Side who are there to guide you.

You may be able to channel the voice of your spirit guide or let the voice of a departed spirit speak through you. You may hear the spirit's message and be able to repeat it word for word. Some people experience a deep altered state of focus in which their voices change and the spirit speaks through them. If you have this talent, it is advisable that you do not have the experience alone. Have someone with you who can assist and guide you through the process.

Internal Sounds and Music

Besides voices, certain sounds may provide you with psychic insights. Some people hear ringing in both or one of their ears that appears as a "heads-up" or "pay attention" notice from the Universe. You may already be receiving some sort of a sound communication without even realizing it. If you have sounds in your head, pay attention to their possible meanings.

Do you hear music in your mind? Have you ever had a song pop into your head and a short time later heard it on the radio or television? If so, what does that mean? It could be your spirit guides telling you to pay attention to other messages that may give you psychic insight. There is always a meaning to the messages, sounds, or music, and sometimes when you hear them you are merely receiving a confirmation to just pay attention in the future.

External Voices, Sounds, and Music

Besides the voices, sounds, and music in your mind, you may be able to actually hear external sounds that others don't pick up. This may be due to very sensitive hearing, much like an animal that hears a sound in the distance long before most humans can. Some of you may be able to hear the sounds of another time period. The sound may be one that has left an impression on the location or on an object. It may also be possible for you to project yourself into the future and hear the sounds of future events.

It's okay not to be able to explain your clairaudience. You may have many clairaudient talents, or you may have one or even none. If the hearing sense is not your strength, another one will be.

You may hear spirits who exist around a particular area. They may try to communicate with you, or they may just go on about their business, re-enacting a scene from their life as if you were not there. You may eavesdrop on a celebration, a dance, an argument, or a battle. All of these activities run their own course on a different plane whether people notice or not.

You may externally hear the voices of your guides, angels, or those who have passed over. They may be a direct communication to and for you. It may be hard to determine if the voice, sound, or music is in your mind or if it is external and heard by your ears. It really doesn't make a difference as long as you accept it as a positive reality. The more you become aware of and trust your ability to hear external voices, the more you will become in tune with your natural psychic intuition.

EXPERIMENT WITH INTERNAL CLAIRAUDIENCE

When you try the clairaudience exercises, you may hear all the different voices, sounds, and music without worrying, for now, about whether they are real. The goal is for you to gather the information first. Once you have done that, you can compile your experiences to see what feels right for you. Developing and honing your psychic talent is essentially the same as developing any artistic ability. It is the combining of your natural talent and the willingness to learn, along with developing the techniques that work best for you. Remember that practice makes perfect.

Exercise: Explore Internal Clairaudience

To begin this exercise, find a comfortable place to relax, either sitting or lying down, where you will not be interrupted for at least half an hour. If you are worried about falling asleep, set an alarm or have someone check on you at the time you wish to end your exercise. You may have someone read the exercise to you, or you may record it in advance and play it back for yourself, or you may read it as you progress, taking as much time as you want.

You may begin by focusing on your breathing. Inhale and exhale slowly, and allow yourself to feel the peace and love of the Universe as you do so. With each breath, you may feel your muscles relax more and more. When you feel any particular muscle stiffen, just let it relax. Let your eyes go out of focus and slowly close as you begin to concentrate on your crown chakra, and let the positive energy flow down to your third-eye chakra.

Now you may feel the energy of your third eye begin to flow as it opens to the loving energy of the Universe. You may feel the peace and love in total balance with your third-eye chakra. You may hear the tone of the energy as it finds its balance. Continue to breathe in and out slowly, and spend a few moments with the love and peace of your third eye as the unconditionally loving energy of the Universe gently encloses you in its protective bubble.

Balance Your Chakras

Now you may begin to work your way down through the rest of your chakras, focusing on your throat chakra next. You may feel the love and peace of the Universe flowing downward to and through your throat energy center. When you feel that this center is balanced, focus on your heart. Continue to repeat the opening and balancing exercise on each chakra until you have opened and balanced your root chakra. After you have completed your balancing exercise, you may turn your focus back to your throat chakra, the center of your clairaudient abilities.

Listen to Your Mind

When you are ready, you may focus on your throat chakra and let your energy center open to any voice, sound, or music that flows through. At first there may be a lot of interference from outside sound stimuli or internal static from your conscious mind. All you need to do is relax and feel the love and peace of the Universe flow through your throat center. Breathe in and out, and let your mind wander. You may become aware of a distant voice, sound, or music.

Let it continue, and focus on hearing it more clearly and turning up the volume if needed.

Identify Your Guides, Spirits, or Angels

You may ask that you hear the voice or voices of your guides, angels, or other spirits. There may be more than one guide, each of whom has a specific purpose in communicating with you. You may get an answer through your own internal voice, or you might hear other voices. You may hear the voice of a loved one who has passed over to the Other Side.

You can ask the name of the voice on the other end. It may be revealed to you, or you may come up with your own name. Do your voices have an agenda for you? If you have a question for the Universal Mind, your guides, or the angels, you may ask and turn it over for an appropriate answer. You may or may not get an answer right away. You may receive insights on world conditions, advice on health issues for others as well as for yourself, or spiritual messages that can help you grow in your knowledge of the Universe.

Dreams You Hear

Do you hear voices in your dreams? Is the voice from your guides, angels, or other spirits? Are the voices from deceased loved ones? Do you hear the voice of God or other divine figures when you dream? Do you receive Universal insights when you are asleep?

Do you hear conversations in your dreams? If so, are you listening to others, or are you participating in the dialogue? Have you ever dreamed a conversation and then experienced it when you were awake? Do you have dreams of conversations from a different time in history, as if you were hearing an event that has already taken place?

Do you hear sounds when you dream? If so, what are they, and what do they mean? Do you dream the same sounds over and over, or do you get different sounds such as water flowing, wind blowing, or natural or mechanical sounds? Can you determine a pattern of events in relationship to sounds that you dream? Are the sounds pleasant or unpleasant?

Many composers hear their compositions in their head before they put them on paper. A composer might wake up in the middle of the night and write down what he just dreamed. Sometimes the music can flow so quickly, it is impossible to capture all the notes.

Do you hear music in your dreams? Is it something you have heard before, or are the melodies entirely new? Do you dream music and then hear it played somewhere at a later time? If you write music, have you ever dreamed the main idea of any of your compositions?

Write Down Your Experiences

While you are in a relaxed state, ask yourself if there are any other kinds of internal clairaudience that you may receive. You may hear intuitive voices that may or may not make sense to you. Remember, you are the information-gatherer at this point in your life map. Even though you may not understand what you hear at the time you receive it, its purpose may become apparent in the future.

Keep writing material close to your bed for insights that come in the night. You may even need a flashlight so you can see to make notes. When you travel, carry a small notepad or diary with you. If you choose to use a recording device to make your notes on, always carry fresh batteries and extra tape or you could also choose to use a digital voice recorder to make your notes.

You may hear the information more than once from both your internal and external sources. As you become more aware of your clairaudience, it is a good idea to keep notes of what you hear internally. You can write down an event after it happens—as soon as you can—making note of the time, date, and your mental, physical, and spiritual condition at the time. Also make note of other details surrounding each situation, including associations with other people, needs that you may have at the time, and even the locations. Keeping track of the regularity of your clairaudience may also prove helpful.

You may find a special place, time, and technique that will provide you with the best and clearest clairaudient experience. Once you have identified your best signal, anchor the state so that you can also use it in different locations. Give yourself a keyword, phrase, or touch to help you connect with your psychic intuition. The more you practice, the easier it will be to enter your clairaudient state.

EXPERIMENT WITH EXTERNAL CLAIRAUDIENCE

When you actually hear voices, sounds, or music that others may not, it is often difficult to get anyone else to believe you really heard something that they didn't. It is always nice to have someone else verify what you have heard, but it is not necessary. The important thing is for you to feel comfortable with your psychic ability to hear more than most others do. For example, you may be able to hear different tone frequencies or much weaker signals than most other people can.

Because the external clairaudience experience can happen without warning, sometimes it might catch you off guard. However, you should always remember that you can take your Belief, the Golden Light of the Universe, and your guides, angels, or other spirits with you wherever you go. You may always feel grounded and safe regardless of any voices, sounds, or music that you hear without warning.

Do you hear any external voices, sounds, or music? If so, do you hear the same thing over and over, or do you hear different sounds, voices, or music? Are there any specific places where you hear these sounds? If so, where are these places, and how well do you hear the sounds? Can you focus on these sounds so that they can become clearer?

Every day, especially first thing in the morning, take the time to find a few moments to center yourself. If you allow yourself to feel in balance with your mind, body, and soul, you will be prepared for external clairaudience.

Can you remember external clairaudience and recall it later in your mind? If so, can you replay the sounds? Can you turn the volume up or down, or slow down or speed up the sounds you first heard externally? Can you remember what you have heard long enough to write it down?

Do you hear sounds from plants? Some people can actually hear a plant make a sound when it needs watering. If you can hear other sounds, what are they? You may hear the sound of energy as it moves through the air. You may hear sounds that relate to emotions emitted by other people or even animals.

Sounds from the Past and Future

Can you visit a location and hear sounds that may have been made there some time before? If so, can you determine when the sounds were made and what was taking place at that time? Do you hear the same sounds at the same location at different times? Can you tell the mood of the sounds? Can you remember these sounds so that you can recall them at a later time?

Do you hear external voices, sounds, or music that relates to the future? If so, do you receive warnings, good news, or even sweepstake numbers? Can you identify the voices, sounds, or music you hear externally? Do they come to you at specific times, places, or locations? Does a voice ever speak to you "out of nowhere" to warn you of impending danger?

BALANCE YOUR VISUAL AND AUDITORY PSYCHIC ABILITIES

Now it's time to combine your clairvoyant and clairaudient abilities to examine how they work together. If you're ready, you will experience your internal psychic seeing and hearing abilities first. Remember that any time you want or need to, you may always return to your conscious mind fully aware of your surroundings, feeling positive and relaxed.

As you learn how to balance and use your clairvoyant and clairaudient abilities, you will begin to rely on them for insights and guidance in your work, relationships, and spiritual development, as well as in other aspects of your life. Be patient, and remember to stay grounded and protected by the loving energy of the Universe. Like any other skill or talent, the more you develop and use your psychic abilities, the more they are ready to work for you.

Exercise: Combine Clairvoyance and Clairaudience

Find a comfortable place, and prepare yourself to experience your Universal golden light trance. Take a deep breath and slowly exhale. Close your eyes, focus on your crown chakra, and feel the positive, loving energy of the Universe begin to flow down to your third-eye chakra. You may allow yourself to open and balance your chakras, taking time to feel the positive, peaceful, and loving energy of the Universe.

Let yourself feel the loving energy of the Universe as it forms a protective bubble around you, and then focus on the psychic energy flow of your third-eye and throat energy centers. When you feel very comfortable and peaceful, you may ask your Belief to experience either a visual image or a sound in your mind that may help you in your psychic development. Be patient. At first the images or sounds may come slowly.

If for any reason you become uncomfortable, you may always stop, take a deep breath, exhale, open your eyes, and come back to your conscious mind relaxed and feeling positive and filled with the peace and love of the Universe.

As you learn to tune in to your psychic flow, it will become easier and easier to connect. You may have a lot of conscious clutter that needs to be filtered out. You can accomplish this by just letting it come and go without trying to control it. If you resist or try to redirect your conscious clutter, you will wind up fighting it rather than stepping aside and letting it flow off into space.

Let any images you have become clearer and clearer with each breath you take. Can you see and hear your image at the same time? Can you change views or raise and lower the volume of the sounds you hear? Can you watch your images as if you were watching a movie or video? Can you replay, slow down, or speed up your images?

Can you receive images in pictures and sound that relate to the future? If so, do they relate to you, to someone you know, or to a larger group of people? Can you be shown and told things that will be helpful to you and/or others in the future? Can you see and hear warnings through your internal images?

Can you experience images and sounds together that are from a different time in history? Perhaps the images are from a past-life memory. Can you project your mind back to a period of history and see and hear what it was like to be there? Can you remember these experiences and replay them later in your mind?

CHAPTER 9

DISCOVER CLAIRSENTIENCE

Clairsentience means "clear feeling." Many people argue that "feeling" is the most important of the five senses, perhaps because it is often combined with one or more of the other senses. Even by itself, feeling can provide a wealth of psychic information. Out of your five main senses, the sense of feeling or the kinesthetic sense is most strongly connected to the memory process. You often feel when you experience images, sounds, smells, or tastes. In this chapter, you will have the opportunity to investigate clairsentience. Your ability to feel is a very important part of the way you process all of your different senses. As you progress through the material, you will learn more about how to determine and develop your clairsentient abilities.

THE POWER OF KINESTHETIC EXPERIENCES

You experience kinesthetically through touch and emotions. You process what you feel both internally and externally. These feelings may relate to the past, present, or future. They may come to you in dreams, during trances, through your mind, or through external touch. It can be very difficult for some people to differentiate their kinesthetic sense from their other senses.

You may be able to feel the emotions of others or the temperature of the weather in a past life. Edgar Cayce was able to project himself to a location he had never been before and report back on weather conditions. Sensing psychic feelings can often be problematic for those who absorb the feelings of others.

Intuitive Touch

Touch is a very powerful sense. When you touch something, it can unleash a flow of psychic images. You may feel repelled or drawn by people or items that you touch. You may be able to feel an aura or energy field around a person, a location, a plant, or an animal. A touch can create a peaceful and secure feeling or evoke anger.

Many intuitive healers get much of their information through touch. Just as you may be able to feel the pull of an underwater current, they can feel the current of energy as it flows through and around a body. Most healers learn how to use their hands to move and balance the energy around others.

There are many different ways that the sense of touch provides you with psychic information. It may be as simple as feeling an energy field around someone. It may be through the use of a dowsing rod or a pendulum when you feel the answer to a question you have asked the Universe. It may be that you can feel a tingle in your hands or a hum in your third eye when you are experiencing a psychic connection. As you are collecting clairsentient information, you might feel a pain, an itch, a tickle, or a pulsating sensation.

You may have a psychic defense system that issues warnings or validations through certain feelings. Even though many originate in your mind, you still may actually feel them externally or physically. Learning how your body produces certain physical feelings that relate to psychic messages can be very helpful as you develop and become comfortable with your intuitive abilities.

If you feel overwhelmed emotionally and are having trouble finding a balance in your life, you should seek out a qualified counselor in your area. Sometimes a person forgets how to close a channel once it is open, and in that case it is advisable to get some help.

The feeling of certain textures can produce psychic images as well. For instance, a certain food texture could trigger a past-life memory. The same thing is true for the texture of something you touch or wear. Textures can suddenly change your focus into an altered psychic state without warning.

Feelings from Objects, Places, or People

Have you ever held or touched an object and gotten a feeling about its past? You may have been able to feel a mood through the object or sense something about the people who have held it before. Just as some people have the ability to see auras, others can sense the auras or energy imprint left on an object or place by those that have previously been exposed to it. If you were affected by a strong mood during a time when you connected to an object, your mood or feelings would have been integrated into the object's energy. There is memory imagery imprinted on just about everything, and yet most people are not aware of the clairsentient information that exists right at their fingertips.

Have you ever been someplace and all of a sudden felt a very strong emotional feeling that was not related to your mood at the time? Have you ever had the feeling in certain locations that ghosts or spirits or something else was watching you? If so, what feelings did you have—happiness, sadness, fear, peace, or something else? When you visit places where you have never been before, do you ever have the feeling that you are "home" again? If you were able to answer many of these questions in the affirmative, you may want to investigate your clairsentient abilities further.

If you take in the emotional baggage of someone else, living or dead, you have become "responsible" for that person. Over a long period of time, the responsibility can affect your health. You can ask your spirit guides for help in getting released from this burden.

Can you think of people you know and sense their mood or state of well-being? Can you look into a person's eyes and feel the essence of his or her soul? Can you feel if someone is sincere or a potential threat? Have you ever met someone for the first time and felt as though the two of you have known each other for your whole lives? All of these feelings come through your psychic abilities of clairsentience.

ABSORBING ENERGY

Do you absorb feelings or emotions from other people, places, or objects? If you do, how do you respond to what you feel? The intuitive ability to feel is a wonderful gift, but it can also be a terrible curse. For those who are extremely open to clairsentience, it's as if feelings have the power to penetrate the very essence of their souls. This statement is true of many artists and healers.

Your psychic gift may be the ability to feel the mental, physical, and spiritual makeup of other people, locations, and time periods, as well as all other things living now or in the past. Once you have absorbed any of these emotions, it can become part of your energy. If you do not have a way of releasing what you have taken in, your energy can be thrown out of balance.

The energy you absorb, positive or negative, can impact your own energy as long as it remains with you in the form it was received. If the energy is positive, it can have a positive effect on your total energy, but negative energy can have a negative effect.

If you are an energy absorber, you are not alone. Many other people do the same thing. A kinesthetic person often seeks to feel good by taking in positive energy, only to find negative instead. In other words, many people see the good in others but do not see the good in themselves. After a few experiences like this, people often try to close down their kinesthetic abilities.

It sometimes takes a little courage to give yourself permission to take the risk of opening up to what you are feeling. It is important to remember to work with your Belief as you begin to trust and develop your clairsentient abilities. Always ask the Universe to allow you to feel what is right and good for you to feel at the time you need to feel it.

EMOTIONS CAN MANIFEST INTO PHYSICAL FEELINGS

Do you ever get an emotional feeling that you also experience as a physical feeling? Perhaps the hair stands up on the back of your neck, or you feel a pain in your neck. Your head might buzz, or you may feel a sudden heaviness in your stomach. Your knees might get weak, or perhaps you get a pain someplace in your body. Perhaps you experience some other kind of cue that lets you know that something is not right.

Sadness can cause you to feel heaviness in your heart chakra. You may feel someone else's energy invading your aura field, the energy that is emitted by your physical, mental, and spiritual bodies. If you are grounded, you may be able to actually feel the protective bubble of Universal Energy deflecting the negative energy.

Not all emotional feelings that you experience are warnings of negative energy. You may get a body feeling that validates to you that something psychic is taking place at that moment. You may feel a buzz of psychic energy in one or more of your chakras. You may get a special feeling when someone is thinking positive thoughts about you. There are many ways in which you can transfer an emotional image into a physical feeling.

WORKING WITH ENERGIES

Part of clairsentience is being able to work with the energy of the Universe. Can you receive Universal Energy and then project it into someone else's aura or body for the purpose of healing? Do others find that you have a calming or healing effect when you touch them? Can you smooth out the energy in the auras of other people? If so, you may be a natural healer.

Is your energy so strong that it affects others without you even realizing it? Do you have trouble keeping wristwatches running? Do you have trouble with your electric appliances, computers, or other electronic items? If so, you may be emitting a very strong psychic energy field. Somehow that has an effect on sensitive electronic equipment.

Can you produce extra strength to move objects when you need to? Do you have the ability to move objects with your mind or by sending energy through your fingers? Many of you may have special strengths that are part of your psychic energy. If you have that gift, you have an opportunity to do a lot of good with your "power" from the Universe.

AN OPEN, BALANCED HEART CHAKRA

The energy center connected to your clairsentient powers is located in the heart chakra. When the heart chakra is open, you are open to the emotional energy from many different sources. You could be taking in the energy from other people, animals, plants, objects, locations, time periods, and ghosts, as well as from those on the Other Side and other forms of energy.

If your heart chakra is out of balance, you take in way too much negative energy, and as a result, you may find your own energy being affected by outside, unwanted influences. If your heart chakra is blocked, you may receive or be aware of very little emotion.

Protection for your clairsentient abilities is extremely important. When your heart chakra is open and unbalanced, you could be overwhelmed with external emotional and internal feelings. They can come from people, locations, dreams, past lives, future events, ghosts, or deceased spirits.

Creative abilities are often at their peak when the chakra centers are open. At those times, artists, writers, musicians, or dancers produce or perform their greatest work. When they are caught up in the energy flow, they are in a state in which their conscious minds are not fully aware of what is taking place. Unfortunately for many, they focus only on the creative flow, and on nothing else, until it has run its course. These altered states of focus in the creative zone may last a short time or may go on for days, placing the artist at risk of losing touch with reality.

When the centers close up again, the creative effort may or may not be complete. If the results are unfinished, there is always the possibility that the centers will not open again to allow completion. If the work is complete, there may be a chance that the chakras will remain closed and that there will be no more works of that kind produced again. It is the ego mind that causes the doubt, not the intuitive trance. If you are balanced, the flow is natural. The creative energy will always be there in its own way, which will always be the correct way for that moment in time.

Exercise: Balance Your Heart Chakra for Clairsentience

You may open and balance your heart chakra with the chakra-balancing exercise. Find a comfortable place to relax and focus on your breathing. Begin by connecting to your crown chakra at the top of your head and let the Universe's unconditionally loving energy flow down to your third-eye chakra.

When you are ready, you may feel this loving energy flowing down through and balancing each of your chakra centers. Spend as much time as you want letting yourself come into balance, and when you are ready, focus on your heart chakra. You may feel yourself totally wrapped in the loving, protective energy of the Universe, safe and secure and ready to investigate your clairsentient abilities.

Investigate Your Clairsentience

From your relaxed state, with your focus on your heart chakra, you may begin to investigate the particular manner in which you receive your intuitive feelings and how you can develop and use them. Do you feel emotions? If so, what kind of emotions do you feel? Can you feel the moods of other people or animals? Can you feel the moods of specific locations or the moods from objects?

Many first-time students of massage, Reiki, or nursing have a great deal of trouble dealing with the physical, mental, and spiritual pain of their clients. The students are absorbers, suddenly thrust into the unbalanced energy of those they are trying to heal. If you are learning hands-on healing arts such as massage or Reiki, it is a good idea to ground yourself often.

Can you feel the moods of spirits or beings who may have died and left unresolved issues on the earth plane? Do you feel emotions about certain events in a different period of history or about the future? Are you overwhelmed with emotions at certain times and don't know why? Do you feel the emotions of family or friends with whom you do not have daily contact? Do you ever get a "gut feeling" that you should contact someone immediately?

You may contemplate these questions as long as you want while you are in your relaxed state, and when you are ready to come back to your conscious mind, you will be fully aware of your surroundings, feeling positive and relaxed. If you are clairsentient, you may find that there are many ways you can find fulfillment in using your abilities to help others. You may want to investigate the study of a healing art such as Reiki or massage. You may be an animal communicator or have the ability to counsel others. If you are clairsentient, you may know more about others than you want to, but as you learn to understand what you are sensing, it can be a very helpful tool in your life.

COMBINING CLAIRSENTIENCE WITH OTHER ABILITIES

Once you gain some understanding of your clairsentient abilities, try combining them with your senses of vision and hearing. As you do so, you will become aware of how these three senses work for you and how they can be used in your psychic development.

Exercise: Combine Your Clairsentience

When you are ready, you may get comfortable and focus on your breathing. Starting with your crown chakra, allow yourself to focus on the flow of the Universe's unconditionally loving energy as it moves down from the top of your head to your third-eye chakra. You may feel this protective energy flowing over and around you as you feel your chakra centers come into balance.

Continue to focus on your third eye, and when you are ready, combine this focus with your throat and your heart chakras. You are now ready to experience images through your senses of sight, hearing, and touch—together. If you have a specific question for the Universe, your guides, or your angels, you may ask it at this time with gratitude, thanking your Source for providing you with the right images. You may give yourself a few moments to let the images form in your mind.

CREATE A PSYCHIC ANCHOR

In nautical terms, an anchor is a device to hold a ship safely in one position. In psychic terms, an anchor is something that brings you back to a state of focus. You can trigger your anchor, or something else can trigger it. Athletes develop anchors to help put them in the "zone." An example is the many different moves baseball players make before they take their place at bat. They are attempting to put themselves into an altered state of focus that helps them perform at their best.

Chances are that you have already been using anchors whether you are consciously aware of them or not. These anchors can either be good or bad for you. Think of love and fear as two opposite types of anchors. The thought of fear can cause people to stiffen, while the thought of something loving can create softness. You can probably think of something that anchors a fear as well as something that puts you in a positive state.

Knowing how to create positive anchors for yourself as well as others can be a powerful tool to help with psychic development. It really isn't a complicated process, and your anchors will be different than anyone else's because they reflect how only your mind works. Creating instant altered states of focus can be a very useful tool in almost every aspect of your life, not just in developing your psychic abilities. You have already started to develop an anchor when you allow yourself to feel the Universe's protective, unconditionally loving energy. It's time now to create a shortcut to that energy that lets you access it in just a moment of time.

Exercise: Create Your Psychic Anchor

To create a psychic anchor, follow the steps used in the chakra-balancing exercise earlier in this chapter. Start from the crown chakra and continue to let the Universe's unconditionally loving energy flow over and around you as you feel each one of your chakra centers opening and balancing. There is no specific time limit. Continue at a pace that is right and good for you.

When you are ready, just let yourself feel the loving energy that wraps around and over you. Let yourself feel safe and protected by the team that goes with and guides you. You may thank your team for the loving support they provide and for the psychic information that they relay to you. With each breath, you feel safe and protected, knowing that whenever you want or need to, you can always come back to full consciousness feeling positive and relaxed.

Now ask that you may receive a word, an idea of something to touch, a mental picture, or just a positive feeling that can bring you instantly back to this altered state of focus where you are immersed in your protective bubble of Universal loving energy. This information may come to you through one or more of your senses. You may see, hear, feel, or—as you will soon learn—taste, or smell your anchor. It could be as simple as taking a breath or touching a thumb and a finger together.

You may receive your information right away, or it may come to you later. You may create a temporary anchor and choose a permanent one when the time is right. If you have not chosen an anchor yet, consider using just a single breath.

For a moment, just feel the Universe's loving energy as you experience what you have chosen for your anchor. Suggest to yourself that every time you connect to your psychic anchor, you will return to this state of altered focus. Suggest to yourself that the more you practice triggering your anchor, the easier it will be, and soon it will trigger itself whenever you need or want to feel the energy surrounding you.

Now take a deep breath and come back to full consciousness. After a moment, try your anchor and let yourself return to your altered state of focus. Take another breath and return again. Try this with your eyes closed and then come back to full consciousness. Now experience it with your eyes open and come back to full consciousness.

Try concentrating on your third eye and going to your altered state of focus and coming back. You can use this while you are fully awake. You will always be aware of what you are doing and what is going on around you. The more you practice, the easier it becomes to trigger your psychic protective anchor.

THE PSYCHIC POWERS OF SMELL, TASTE, AND TOUCH

Smell and taste play an important part in the way you receive your psychic images. In fact, you may have been using these senses all along without even knowing it. They are both very powerful senses that can instantly place you into an altered state of focus with no previous warning. Combined with the other senses, they can help you access your psychic abilities. Touching an object can also trigger psychic visions or emotions. For example, some people can touch an antique table and be able to tell something about its history and the people who once owned it. This is called psychometry. In this chapter you will explore your senses of smell and taste in terms of how they impact your psychic abilities and you will continue your psychic development by practicing your psychometric abilities.

THE STRONG IMPACT OF SMELL

Your sense of smell may be a very important part of your psychic abilities. Some people have no sense of smell or for some reason have lost that ability. Some people have very sensitive noses that make it hard for them to tolerate even the smallest amount of an unwanted aroma.

Even the recollection of a smell can place a person back into a memory where they had encountered the smell before. These, of course, could be either positive or negative images from their past.

To effectively use your sense of smell, you first need to understand how you have been using it in your life. Just as all the other senses, you may find that smell has had more of an impact on you than you might have imagined. As you consider your smell sense, remember that you do not have to bring back and experience any negative smells from the past.

Some people have the ability to develop images by experiencing one or more smells that are imprinted on an object. The smell imprint could be strong enough for most people to recognize or so faint that only those with the most acute sense of smell will notice it. Smell imprints may be connected to a person or to a physical location. Later in this chapter you will have the opportunity to investigate your sense of smell through an exercise in psychometry.

Smell Sources

Sometimes the imprint of a smell may span a long period of time. If the object is a hundred years old, it has been collecting smell imprints for a hundred years. For example, when Jess examined an old canning jar found in the woods, she instantly experienced the smell of cider. Perhaps a laborer from a different time had brought a drink to his work to keep him refreshed during the day. To the normal nose, this peek into history would have been overlooked.

A geographic location can hold the imprints of smells that flow back through history. Imagine what it would be like to suddenly be drawn into a battle as you catch the smell of gunpowder while strolling through a historical site. The smells may even trigger your other senses to put you into an altered state of consciousness so powerful that you are actually there, seeing the fighting, hearing the sounds, and feeling the emotions experienced by the participants. Some people experience time travel because of their sense of smell.

Smell As a Method to Receive Messages

Not only is your sense of smell a way for you to enter into a psychic altered state, it can also be a way of receiving communication from the Other Side. Have you ever experienced a smell in the air that reminded you of someone you knew that had passed? It could be the smell of fresh flowers, pipe smoke, perfume, or coffee brewing. These smells can materialize at a time in your life when a little support from a loved one is really appreciated.

When more than one person has the same experience at the same time, such as a whiff of perfume or the smell of a cigar in a location where there is no explanation for the source, it may mean that something paranormal is taking place, especially if not everyone present is experiencing the smell. It is possible that those imagining the smell in their minds may be having a psychic experience.

You may be a medical intuitive through your sense of smell. Some people have the ability to determine the health of others by reading their odor. The subject may have a healthy smell or one that signals bad health. You may have already noticed this, but have not been able to pinpoint the exact meaning. Someone with medical training and good smell ability may be able to understand the medical cause of the odor they have experienced.

As you can see, there are many ways that the sense of smell can figure into the psychic images that you receive on a daily basis. You may have thought of even more examples of how you are affected by smells. It is time for an exercise to help you remember how smells may have already played an important role in your life. Remember that it is possible that you do not process images through the sense of smell.

Exercise: Psychic Smell

Find a comfortable spot, take a few relaxing breaths, and try out your psychic anchor to help you enter into a positive altered state of consciousness. Remember that, at any time for any reason, you may take a deep breath and return to full consciousness totally aware of your surroundings. Allow yourself to feel the positive, unconditionally loving energy of the Universe flowing over and around you. Take a moment and enjoy this relaxing experience.

* When you are ready, feel this positive energy flowing over your crown chakra and downward to your third-eye chakra.

* Let the energy continue to flow on down to your throat and heart chakras, down to your solar-plexus chakra, sacral or belly chakra, and to your root chakra.

* Feel yourself immersed in the unconditionally loving energy of the Universe, safe and secure.

* Look back into your memories to determine how you have experienced the sense of smell in your life.

* Let a positive memory come to the surface of your conscious mind, and see the images in your mind's eye.

Can you imagine being in the image? Are there any sounds? What is the temperature, and what is your mood? Are there any smells? Can you move around in the image and experience different smells? Can you focus in on one certain smell and get closer to it or move further away?

Take as much time as you want to focus on this image. When you are ready, let yourself return to a positive altered state of focus, surrounded by your positive, loving, and protective Universal Energy. You may now ask your unconscious mind to bring to the surface memories of how you have experienced your sense of smell in the past. Just relax and let these images come to you at a rate that is right and good for you.

Do you remember any smells connected with unexplained events you may have experienced in your life? If so, and if you are comfortable, take a little time to examine one of them. Think of the situation as it unfolded. Can you get a visual, auditory, or feeling image to go with the smell? Are there any other psychic encounters that included the sense of smell?

Take a little time to process this exercise, and when you are ready, slowly come back to a positive and relaxed state of consciousness, fully aware of your surroundings.

You may want to take notes on the information you collected during this exercise. You may have gotten a lot of images related to smell, or it is possible that you didn't experience any. Every mind is different, and how you receive your psychic images will be different than anyone else. The insight you gain into your mind's processes will help you to identify and develop your psychic abilities.

Further Questions to Ponder

Are there any other ways that your sense of smell has brought you psychic information? Take a moment to explore these questions:

* Have you ever had a smell come to you as a warning of something negative? If so, have you had more than one experience of this kind? Perhaps it was a smell connected to a person or a place. Perhaps it was a smell that just materialized out of thin air. What is the earliest experience related to smells that you can remember?

* Have you ever experienced smells related to someone that has passed over to the Other Side? If so, how many times have you had these experiences, and what kind of smells were they? How often and when do they come to you? Can you recognize any pattern in your life that relates to when those smells appear?

* Have you ever experienced dreams in which you could remember the smells? If so, how often do they take place? Are the dreams recurring, or are they always different? Do they have a recurring theme? Do these dreams relate to other time periods in history?

* Have you ever received information on a person's health by the odor they projected? Can you have this experience at will, or does it happen randomly and without warning? When you receive information about others' health through your sense of smell, do any of your other image senses become involved? If so, which of your senses works best for you?

TASTES CAN TRIGGER PSYCHIC IMAGES

Taste is also an important factor in the psychic mix. You may have very sensitive taste buds and imagery, or you may not have much of a sense of taste at all. Just as with the other senses, you will experience taste differently than anyone else.

Perhaps the taste of a certain food can trigger images in your mind. A taste may bring back memories from your childhood that may be positive or negative depending on your experiences at that time. You may relate tastes to certain moods. Perhaps there are tastes that make you happy and tastes that make you sad.

It is possible for certain tastes to trigger past-life memories. You may be flooded with images that have no conscious connections to your current lifetime. Certain foods may cause you to imagine living in a different time period. It is very possible that memories of food stored in your unconscious mind can act as a bridge to help you discover your past.

The taste sense can sometimes be confused with the sense of feeling. Often people will dislike food because of the way it feels in their mouth rather than how it tastes to them. Perhaps you can think of certain foods that you dislike for more than just the taste.

The experience of tasting and eating food can bring about an altered state of consciousness. So, too, can the memory of the taste of food. Even if you have a weak sense of taste, you may be able to recall certain tastes that still exist in your mind. Your taste memories can also be the source of psychic information that you may have been overlooking.

Just as some people get a negative feeling in their gut, others may get a bad taste in their mouth. You may experience the sense of a bad taste when someone around you is not trustworthy or when your guidance team does not agree with something you are considering doing. You may recognize a bad taste of a certain food you do not care for, or the taste you experience may be hard to describe, other than sour or acidic.

Of course, you may also experience a pleasant taste when you are involved in a positive situation. It could be a taste you relate to happy memories. It may be a signal from your team that you are on the right track or that you are connecting with a good person.

Your sense of taste may also create psychic images connected with the health of others. A sour taste in your mouth when you're near someone else may indicate that person has a health problem. A good taste could indicate that everything is well with that person.

THE ART OF PSYCHOMETRY

Psychometry is the ability to gather information imprinted on an object throughout its history. Psychics are able to touch or hold an item and determine who has been connected to it before. It is even possible to determine the places it has been and the events it has witnessed.

Some people find that they take on the emotions that have been imprinted on the object. Others may get vivid pictures in their mind. You may hear sounds, experience smells, or even get a taste in your mouth connected to an object. The way you receive your information will be different than anyone else's. The more you practice, the more you will learn to trust the images you pick up.

How do you know that you are not just imagining rather than getting actual information? Think of it this way: The images in your mind come from somewhere. Are they memories of experiences you can remember or are they something that you just made up? Many people dismiss psychic information as just imagination. What you think you may be imagining could very well be your psychic ability providing you information.

When you begin to practice the psychic development exercise, it is okay to just "imagine." Let the images flow, as long as they do not overwhelm you, without trying to consciously judge what you are "imagining." Your critical mind can get in the way of collecting psychic information when it starts to play judge. Regardless of what comes through your mind, just give it a voice. You can be the judge after the information has been collected and the exercise is over.

When you first practice psychometry, as well as other psychic development exercises, it is a good idea to find someone to be your partner. In fact, when several people experience psychometry together with the same items, it is a great way to compare results and to help you begin to validate your psychic abilities. Just as it is when learning any new skill, it is the practice that helps hone your natural talents.

When you begin to practice psychometry, choose items with a history that's unknown to you. When you work with one or more persons, ask each one to bring several objects with a known history. You can do the same. An item can be passed around or, if it is too big, touched by everyone there. After spending a few moments with it, make notes on the information that came to you in your mind.

When everyone is finished, share what each one picked up. Look for information that is similar from different people. Be careful not to reveal the actual history of the object until after everyone has finished sharing. Reading items such as jewelry, old clothing, or other antiques is a good way to get started. You may be surprised at how your "imagination" compares with everyone else's and the actual history of the object and who had been its owner. Remember, if you do not get the same information as others, it may mean your psychic abilities are in a different area than psychometry.

After you have built up your confidence in psychometry, give it a try on objects with no known history. You might even take an organic item, such as a piece of fruit, and let it take you back through the history of its life, back to when it was just a seed. Try your skills out in nature and see if you can trace the history of the landscape. The art of psychometry can be a useful tool in many aspects of your daily life.

Exercise: Try Psychometry

It is best to practice with other people, but if you are by yourself, that can also work. Ask each participant to bring one or more items of which only they know the history. If you are alone, try to borrow some unfamiliar items that someone else knows about. Find a comfortable location where you can hold or touch each of the items.

Using your psychic anchor, take a deep breath and let yourself drift into your altered state of focus. Let the unconditionally loving energy of the Universe flow over and around you as you ask your guides to provide you with the right psychic images connected to the items you will be touching or holding. When you are ready, allow yourself to open to the energy that has been imprinted on one of the items. Just be one with it for a moment and let the images come to you through your five senses.

Open your mind to whatever information comes to you without analyzing what you are receiving. Remember, if you are getting any unsettling images that make you uncomfortable, you can always set the item down, take a deep breath, and return to consciousness, fully aware of your surroundings. You may also amplify or reduce the intensity of the images you receive depending on how your mind processes in your five senses. Ask yourself these questions:

* ✳ What senses are providing you with images about the item?

* ✳ Do you get pictures about the owners or the people that possessed it?

* ✳ Can you see where the item has been?

* ✳ What is the strongest image?

* ✳ Can you imagine any sounds?

* ✳ How do you feel emotionally about the item?

* ✳ Can you experience traces of smell that have been imprinted?

* ✳ Do you recognize anything relating to taste?

When you have finished reading the item, make some notes about the images you received. If there are more items, repeat the process and go on to the next. When you have finished, return to your fully conscious state and compare results.

CHAPTER 11

ASTRAL PROJECTIONS AND OTHER OUT-OF-BODY EXPERIENCES

Have you ever had an out-of-body experience? Perhaps you left your body in a dream or felt the sensation in your waking life—which can be frightening indeed if it is unexpected. If you have ever had the feeling of leaving your body or are just interested in the concept, then this chapter will give you the opportunity to learn about and experience astral projection through physical or mental out-of-body experiences. You'll also explore how to handle situations if someone enters your psychic space uninvited and how to communicate through mental telepathy.

WHAT IS ASTRAL PROJECTION?

Chances are that at some time in your life, you experienced the sensation that a part of you was leaving your body and that you were flying through space. It could have happened when you were asleep, or it may have happened when you were awake. If you can remember an event like this, then you have had an out-of-body experience, otherwise known as astral projection.

Edgar Cayce practiced astral projection in many of his readings. He would go out into the Universe to the Akashic Book of Records and review the history of the soul that he was doing a reading on. He also traveled to the location of many of the subjects who would request readings through the mail. He even seemed to be able to travel through the subject's body and see the medical problems the person had.

There are many theories about what takes place during an out-of-body experience. Some believe that there is some form of energy that leaves the body and goes elsewhere. The destination could be on the earth plane or in some other dimension. It could be a time long past, or it could be the future. It may be far away—even in distant galaxies—or it may be heaven.

A Soul's Memory

Imagine, for a moment, that in the very beginning of your soul you were conceived from energy at the center of the Universe. You were nothing but a wisp of pure energy, perfectly balanced as both male and female. Within you was the imprint of all the knowledge of the Universe, the past, the future, and the present. Your soul was free to travel wherever its path took it through thought and the Universe's grand design.

There was, and still is, a grand plan for your soul's purpose, which includes gaining experiences with each incarnation to match the knowledge already imprinted in your soul. Each lifetime has a plan and an opportunity to move beyond the lessons that you have chosen to experience. Besides your life plan, you also have something called "free will," and that can make your journey a little more complicated. Free will is your ability to make choices in your life that will either follow your plan or lead you away from it.

Shamans from many different cultures have traveled to other dimensions through their out-of-body experiences. In an altered state of consciousness, a shaman can travel through the earth, the sky, and the underworld. To help them perform the journey, shamans use guides, animal helpers, or even psychedelic drugs.

You may have memories in your soul of lives on other planets and in different types of life forms, not just human. You may have memories of flying through space without restrictions. Those old experiences are still in your soul's memories, and they can actually surface without warning, shifting you into an altered state of consciousness, and you may find yourself flying again.

Near-Death Experiences

Another form of out-of-body experience is the near-death experience. Have you ever had a near-death experience? Many who are revived from a near-death state relate similar experiences of floating free of their bodies and observing what is happening to them from above. They may also feel as if they are being pulled toward a light, or they may see images from their lives in front of their eyes. People having this type of experience often say that they suddenly had the sensation of being pulled back into their bodies and coming back to life.

More often than not, survivors of a near-death experience are never quite the same afterward. Their five senses are often changed and are much more sensitive than they were before. This change results in a sort of state of hyperawareness that causes them to respond differently to life situations than they did before. The experience can cause them to see life from a completely new perspective.

If you would like to read more about near-death experiences, one of the first books on the subject is *Life after Life* by Dr. Raymond Moody. The book relates similar stories by patients of what happened between the time they were declared clinically dead and the time they were revived.

It is not known exactly what transpires in a near-death experience, any more than we know what happens during other out-of-body experiences. Some nurses who have the ability to see energy claim they can see the soul leave a body after it physically dies. Terminally ill patients that lapse in and out of coma have told of meeting loved ones on the Other Side.

TYPES OF ASTRAL PROJECTION

Astral projection may be experienced either as an observer or as actually being there. The experience can occur spontaneously or by consciously projecting yourself to a specific location.

Let's look at the physical out-of-body experiences first. These experiences involve transportation of your physical form so that you have actual physical experiences of sight, sound, feelings, taste, and smell. A physical out-of-body experience can be very powerful. Before attempting astral projection, make sure you are balanced and grounded and are accompanied by your team of spiritual guides or angels.

It is also possible for your mental body to separate from your physical body. With this type of out-of-body experience, you would not feel your body traveling with you. You would be more of an observer than a participant. When you come back, you might remember your out-of-body experience in the form of new wisdom, insight, or visions.

Before you try astral projection, make sure you are very comfortable with the technique and that you trust in your team to keep you safe for your out-of-body experiences. And always remember that you may always come back to consciousness at any time.

Spontaneous Astral Projection

Some of your out-of-body experiences may occur spontaneously. In such cases, you have no warning before suddenly finding yourself on some type of astral plane. You may be transported out of your physical body, or you may feel your physical body itself lifting up. You may find yourself suspended in midair or in a specific location, which you may or may not recognize.

A spontaneous out-of-body experience usually causes a great deal of concern to an unwitting participant. It can first happen at any time, and if you have no knowledge of what astral projection is, you will be totally unprepared. You may have had such an experience, and you may now live in fear that it will happen again. These spontaneous experiences often happen when you are ungrounded and in a state of some sort of confusion. It is during this unbalanced state that you are open to thoughts or experiences that trigger your unconscious memories of when you used to "fly," and the result is often an out-of-body experience.

If you have experienced spontaneous out-of-body experiences before, and you worry about them happening again, develop a technique to keep yourself grounded and always connected to your

Universal team, surrounded by unconditional love. Give yourself a keyword or an anchor that can bring you instantly back.

Learn to recognize the conditions that help produce your spontaneous out-of-body experiences. If you are aware of what takes place just before you feel yourself leaving, you can interrupt the astral projection and bring yourself back to consciousness.

Planned Out-of-Body Experiences

You may decide that you want to practice and perfect the art of traveling outside your body. The more you prepare yourself physically, mentally, spiritually, and emotionally, the more you will be in tune with your experiences. The better you take care of your physical body with proper diet and exercise, the better prepared you will be to handle the exertion that astral travelers sometimes feel.

Being in the proper mental, spiritual, and emotional frame of mind is very important for an out-of-body experience. If you are out of balance, confused, or focused on anything but peace and unconditional love, your trip may not be as successful as if you were ready for the adventure. It is important to develop a trust in your team to watch over you and guide you. Remember, you may go where you want to go, or you may wind up in a place where you are supposed to be.

EXPLORING MIND TRAVEL

Before you try astral projection, you need to know that each person experiences it differently. That's a result of differing mental makeup and sensory perception abilities. When you have an out-of-body experience, you may not be able to process your experience in all five senses—and that's okay. You have a natural psychic ability that is part of your soul's heritage, and the way it provides you with information is different from anyone else on earth. Knowing how your senses can work for you may help give you a better experience in astral projection.

Exercise: Astral Projection

If you're ready, find a comfortable place to sit or lie down. You may want to try placing your body in a position that feels as though at any time you could be floating on your back. Lying on your back with your arms and legs spread apart may help produce the feeling of flying or floating on water.

GET READY:

* You may begin by breathing in and out slowly. Continue to take nice deep breaths as you feel yourself relaxing more and more. You may experience muscles that are stiff and muscles that are relaxed. Every time you feel a muscle stiffen up, you may relax it, as your entire body relaxes more and more.

* You may now let your eyes close and focus on your third eye. As you connect, allow the peace and love of the Universe to flow through your crown chakra and down to your third-eye chakra.

* Take a moment to enjoy this special feeling of peace and love as you continue to breathe in and out slowly. You may allow yourself to feel the peaceful, unconditionally loving energy of the Universe begin to flow down over your body.

* As it works its way downward, you may feel the golden light and loving energy balance the energy flow through each of your centers: the throat, the heart, the solar plexus, the navel, and the root.

* When you are ready, let the loving energy flow in and out of your body as your crown chakra opens to Universal guidance. Let yourself feel the protective energy of the Universe totally surrounding your earthly body.

* Focus on your third eye, and feel the presence of your team grounding you and providing a secure connection to your earthly ties. You may feel safe and secure and fully protected by your team. Let all of your five senses become aware as you experience peace and love and prepare to float up and safely leave your body.

When you are ready, allow yourself to focus on your earthly connection, knowing that you can return any time you want to as you continue to feel safe and secure.

LIFT OFF:

* Let yourself feel the peaceful energy and strength of the Universe slowly lifting you upward. You may experience this with all your senses—sight, hearing, touch, taste, and smell—knowing you are safe and secure with your protective Universal team.

* Let yourself float up a little at first, and feel both the lightness of your body and the positive connection to the ground and to the Universe.

* Look around and experience your new surroundings in all five senses.

* Now let yourself float upward in the atmosphere. You may be aware that you are traveling through a tunnel or following a beam of light. You may ask that you go where you will be shown new insights that relate to your life map and your soul's purpose.

* Take some time to get acclimated. Let your five senses come into focus as you prepare to investigate.

You may not feel your entire body lifting up. You may feel only your mental body as it leaves your physical body. In other words, you may feel a physical out-of-body experience or a mental out-of-body experience. One type of travel may work better for you than the other.

NOW COME BACK:

✻ When you are ready to come back to your body again, take a deep breath, and exhale.

✻ Feel the unconditionally loving energy of the Universe flowing over and around you.

✻ Allow yourself to slowly journey back to your physical body and conscious mind.

✻ Suggest to yourself that you will remember the experiences you had while traveling through time and space.

✻ Now come back to the surface of your conscious mind, fully aware of your physical body and conscious mind, feeling positive and relaxed.

Exercise: Mental Astral Projection

To try mental astral projection, follow the same technique of relaxing, breathing, connecting to the Universal Flow, and opening and balancing your chakras. Once you feel centered and in tune, focus on your crown chakra and let the peaceful, loving energy of the Universe flow down to your third eye. You may feel this incredible, protective energy flowing over and around your body. Allow your mind to travel upward into the atmosphere. You will feel complete freedom as you let yourself go higher and higher, feeling safe and protected by your team.

Always give yourself a suggestion when you are in your altered state of consciousness that all you have to do to stop the experience is follow your connection back to earth, take a deep breath, exhale, and open your eyes to be once again fully conscious, surrounded by positive, peaceful, and loving energy.

You may journey out to the Akashic Book of Records or to other spiritual realms. You may go to a specific destination and observe the events that are taking place. You may visit time periods from the past or the future. You may meet with the masters of the collective unconsciousness in order to ask them for guidance in your life. When you're ready, you may return to your conscious world, fully aware of your surroundings and filled with the peace and love of the Universe.

Practice with a Friend

You might want to arrange to visit a friend through astral projection. Pick a time, and then try out your technique. You might not get a clear image at first, but be patient. Experience the visit in all of your five senses. When you have finished, make notes of what you experienced and check with your friend to see how close you were.

You can try both physical and mental astral projection. You can reverse roles and let your friend visit you. You may want to pick a place to meet and project yourselves there. You might try meeting in a past life or in the future. As you do, be sure to remember to always keep yourself surrounded by your Universal Energy and connected to your team.

UNWANTED PSYCHIC GUESTS

Have you ever seen a physical image of someone who is in the same place as you, but you know that it is impossible for him or her to really be there? Sometimes it's just a very strong feeling that someone is there, or you may hear a voice or experience a smell. Perhaps they have come to visit you on an astral plane. They may have a presence so powerful that you actually see an impression of them. Their visit may be welcome, but that isn't always the case.

It is possible for you to experience someone or something visiting you through astral projection just as you can visit others. Those who aren't expecting this often feel defenseless when it happens.

They do not know how to stop other energies from entering their space.

Some people are more at risk from psychic invaders than others. You may already have a natural psychic defense system, like your golden bubble, guides, angels, or other beings that fend off unwanted visitors. But if you are vulnerable or unbalanced and let your protective guard down, you could be open to psychic invaders. These visitors might not mean harm, but they have no sense of someone's privacy. They can rob you of your sense of self.

Safeguarding Yourself

If unwanted psychic guests are a problem for you, there are some basic steps to take that will help you deal with them:

* Trust in your protective team to keep you grounded and immersed in the positive and unconditionally loving energy of the Universe.

* Keep yourself balanced physically, mentally, spiritually, and emotionally.

* Stay in constant communication with your guides, angels, or other spirits.

* Listen to your inner guidance system.

* Pay attention to what is taking place both around and inside you.

* If you sense an invasion, ask your team to intervene.

There may be times when you want to have visitors. If that's the case, set up a time and ask them to join you.

It is also possible for you to have visitors while you are in your dream state. If you go to sleep unbalanced, you may be opening yourself to unwanted invaders. The best protection is to use the same safeguarding techniques before you go to sleep. If you develop a protection anchor, you can trigger it just before you go to sleep and suggest that it will stay with you after you have drifted off.

Many people travel in dreams. You may be more successful lifting off when you're sleeping than when you're awake. You may go places in your dreams that you actually plan to visit in the future.

EXPLORING MENTAL TELEPATHY

Mental telepathy is communication on a mental level between two or more people or between people and animals. Mental telepathy is a form of clairsentience, or psychic perception of feelings. You might pick up on the emotions of a close friend or family member and suddenly know you need to contact that person. You may be able to hear what someone else is thinking. You may be able to step into someone else's mind and see what they are seeing.

Law enforcement agencies have profilers who attempt to put themselves in the mind of the criminal so that they may gain valuable insights that will help police solve the crime. They work with known clues to help them fill in the blanks. On the other end of the spectrum, there are others with incredible gifts in telepathy that they choose to use for their own gain. These people attempt to control others—strangers or people they know—by using their psychic abilities.

In the 1980s, the U.S. Army created a special group of psychic remote viewers to help keep an eye on the country's enemies. The participants received map coordinates and were asked to project themselves to certain locations and report their observations. Unfortunately, once Congress discovered that the military was using psychics, the funding ended, and the program was terminated.

Try reading minds with a friend or relative. One of you should go somewhere separate from the other, like into another room, and concentrate on an object, a word, or a symbol, while the other tries to learn what it is. Try up to five different items, one at a time, and then see how you did. You may be able to picture, hear, or feel what the correct answer is. Use your focus technique to prepare for the experiment.

CHAPTER 12

MEDIUMS AND SPIRIT COMMUNICATION

All matter, including spiritual matter, is connected on some level or another. Because of this, some individuals called mediums can connect with images from the past or future as well as with ghosts and spirit guides, and use that knowledge to help the living. In this chapter, you will learn what a medium is and the different ways mediums can use their gifts to communicate with the Other Side. You will have the opportunity to understand the various ways that spirits can communicate through people and to see if you have the ability to connect with them. Once you learn how to safeguard yourself, you'll have a chance to try an exercise in mediumship and to experience what it is like to do a reading.

WHAT IS A MEDIUM?

All mediums are psychic, but not all psychics are mediums. So what is the difference? Mediums can generally do all the things that psychics do, such as connecting with images from the past and the future, as well as seeing auras and energies, like ghosts. They may have healing powers and the ability to read the minds of others. Not all psychics, however, communicate directly with spirits, which is a distinguishing quality of mediums.

Communication with those who have died, and with other kinds of spirits, has been a practice since the early history of humans. Many cultures sought out spirits for guidance through their prophets, witch doctors, oracles, soothsayers, or medicine men and women, to name a few. Modern mediumship gained popularity through the spread of a religious movement in the latter half of the nineteenth century known as Spiritualism.

As defined by the National Spiritualist Association of Churches, "Spiritualism is the Science, Philosophy, and Religion of continuous life, based upon the demonstrated fact of communication, by means of mediumship, with those who live in the Spirit World."

Mediums are thought to enter into a trance state or altered state of consciousness that is deep enough to allow spirits to communicate directly through them. Mediums are often unaware of what is happening during the process. This differs from the usual lighter altered states of consciousness that psychics experience when doing readings. Psychics are usually aware of their physical surroundings as well as the images they are receiving in their mind. That said, many of today's mediums who do group readings are aware of their surroundings while they are passing on messages from the Other Side.

So, who can be a medium? Anyone who has the ability to connect to the spirit world through various levels of altered states of consciousness. Remember that every person's mental makeup is different. This means that if you are a medium, you have always been one and may not have known it until now—or may not know until you have finished this chapter. It comes back to the concept that all matter, including spiritual matter, is connected on some level or another.

The Spiritualist Church continues to promote mediumship training and incorporates readings and healings as a regular part of their Christianity-based worship services. Once certified, a medium is expected to continue to work on and improve her abilities.

TYPES OF MEDIUMSHIP

There is more than one way to communicate with the dead and with other spirits. A person may communicate through physical mediumship, mental mediumship, trance mediumship, direct voice, and channeling. In the following sections you will learn about physical mediumship, trance mediumship, and channeling. You may find that one of these ways is better for you than another.

Physical Mediumship

Physical mediumship was the most popular form of spirit communication during the time of the famous Fox sisters who communicated through rapping with the spirit of a man thought to have been murdered and buried in the cellar of their cottage. A rapping system of communication was used to answer questions. One rap would mean "yes," and two raps would mean "no." Some of the events even produced evidence of the spirit's energy in the form of a mist-like substance known as ectoplasm.

Mediums who practiced physical mediumship would provide a connection with the deceased's loved ones or other entities that allowed the spirit to manifest physical evidence, which proved there was communication taking place with the spirit. Participants and witnesses would often hear loud knocks, rapping, or other noises thought to be manifested through the spirit.

The Fox sisters, Kate (1837–1892) and Margaretta (1833–1893), brought the Spiritualist movement to the forefront. The sisters claimed that they were able to manifest spirit communication through the rappings of a peddler who had been murdered and whose bones were found in the Fox home. The public became enthralled as the sisters gave demonstrations of this "psychic" manifestation throughout the country. In 1888, the sisters confessed that the rappings had been a hoax and that they had produced the rappings of the murdered peddler by cracking their toe and knee joints.

Mediums in the latter part of the 1800s were usually women, and the spirit communication might take place in dimly lit rooms, which were thought to help provide a stronger connection. The medium would use devices such as levitation tables and spirit trumpets for the spirits to make their presence known. As time went on, investigators into this phenomenon of physical mediumship found that many of the mediums, including the Fox sisters, were actually using trickery to fool their clients. The public lost interest, and the fad faded.

Today there is a renewed interest in physical mediumship and spirit manifesting. Spirit photography has entered the digital age and is very popular with ghost hunters. Another way to communicate is through table-tipping. The medium and one or more people sit around a three-legged table and summon the presence of departed loved ones. With hands placed palms down on the table, the table usually begins to move and even appears to dance when the spirit comes through, confirming that the departed is still present.

Trance Mediumship

Trance mediumship is a much more popular form of mediumship and is widely used today. Trance mediumship is an altered state of consciousness in which the medium is always aware of his or her physical surroundings while receiving messages from spirits.

Some mediums may only experience the trance imagery in one sense, while another medium may have the use of all five. Some mediums work harder at receiving the information, while others seem to tune in to messages from the Other Side that are clear and to the point.

Some mediums will see the deceased and be able to give a full description of how they look. Some see symbols, such as a rose, that means something specific to the medium. Some will see the connection to the Other Side in a certain position behind or beside the subject of the reading. The position may indicate the deceased's relationship to the subject.

What Can a Medium See?

There are many ways that a trance medium can communicate visually with the Other Side. Mediums may see the deceased as they were at a younger age or possibly at the time of their death. Some mediums can step into the memory of a spirit and relate exactly how that person felt during that experience. It is also possible to see the spirit guide or angel of the reading's subject.

What Can a Medium Hear?

Trance mediums may also have the ability to hear what the deceased want to say. They could receive messages that relate to events when the deceased were alive, such as an explanation of how they died or a reminder of something special in their relationship with the message recipient. They may have advice for the ones left on earth. A medium may not actually hear the spirit's voice. Sometimes mediums simply know what spirits are communicating, or they get the message through a spirit guide.

What Can a Medium Feel?

Some mediums are empathic and feel what the spirits may have felt while they were alive. Sometimes their bodily sensations will tell them how a person died. Mediums may be able to feel or sense the moods spirits felt while they were alive, or they might be able to read the emotions spirits have on the Other Side.

What Can a Medium Smell?

Some spirits make their presence known by presenting a medium with a smell. These smells could be anything from tobacco smoke or perfume, to something baking in an oven. Sometimes mediums recognize the smell, and sometimes they can only describe what it seems like. Often the smell will be significant for the person getting the reading.

What Can a Medium Taste?

Some mediums will experience a taste when communicating with a deceased loved one. The taste could indicate a favorite food the spirit enjoyed when still alive. Each medium communicates with the dead differently.

Channeling

Another form of mediumship is channeling. A medium who channels enters into a deep trance or altered state of consciousness in which he loses total awareness of his surroundings. The spirit speaks directly through the medium and takes over control of the dialogue. This spirit is known as a "spirit operator."

The medium will often become stiff and rigid when the spirit operator takes over. The medium's voice can even change to that of the spirit, making it a somewhat scary experience for the unsuspecting. In these cases, the spirit often desires a platform for its words of wisdom.

> The spirit operator can usually be communicated with directly. Questions can be asked of the spirit, who then often offers wisdom of Universal proportions. Some famous channels include Jane Roberts, whose spirit operator was Seth; Esther Hicks, who channels Abraham; and Lee Carroll, who channels Kryon.

It is possible to use hypnosis to induce an individual into a deep trance. Someone who acts as a conductor to help facilitate the altered state could help create the trance, or it could be self-induced. The conductor can ask the desired questions once the medium has entered an altered state. At the end of the session, the conductor can then help bring the medium out of the trance and back to full consciousness. Edgar Cayce would place himself in a hypnotic trance and then answer questions posed to him by the person conducting the session.

The exercises in this book will focus on trance mediumship. It is much easier to investigate your natural abilities to communicate with the dead or spirits when you are in a light trance or altered state of consciousness, fully aware of your surroundings. You might think of that state as being involved in a daydream or totally focused on your imagination. You will have a chance to identify your mediumship skills later in this chapter.

KEEP GROUNDED TO SAFEGUARD YOURSELF

As you identify and develop your mediumship abilities, you will see why it is important to keep yourself grounded in that loving

Universal Energy. The more you experiment and investigate the world of a medium, the more you will open to communication from those who have passed over and other spirits who want their messages to be heard. You may feel their emotions or their pain. You may see scenes in your mind that you are unprepared to witness. You may hear the voices of the dead, or experience smells or tastes that appear suddenly.

As you open to the Other Side, you could become like a light in the dark that attracts insects on a warm summer night. In other words, you may become a draw for spirits wanting to communicate through you.

One medium on the West Coast suddenly found that she had become a magnet for many of the dead of Hurricane Katrina in New Orleans. They were looking for a way to communicate with their loved ones. Unfortunately, she lived far away from the disaster and was powerless to help those from the Other Side get their messages through.

Another medium used to attract unwanted spirits until she started repeating a small daily prayer. She used her Belief to help her stay surrounded by loving energy and connected with only the spirits that were right for the occasion when she entered her altered state of focus. If you have not developed your positive anchor to your Belief, you may want to review that section in this book as you get ready to investigate mediumship.

How do you keep spirits in line? Spirits are like people, and they may have the same personality they had when they were alive. Some are pushy and want to get in the front of the communication line, while others may not want to come through at all. Some faiths do not believe in the spiritual world, and dead people of that faith may feel uncomfortable about being contacted on the Other Side.

There are spirits who have been seeking the light for a while, and they may not want to let go of your light. Once they have found their voice through you, they may not want to give up the podium. That is a good reason for "trance channelers" to have a control that helps bring them back out of their deep altered state of consciousness. Always remember that you are the boss of your own mind, and you can decide when and with whom you want to communicate.

Before you begin to communicate with the Other Side, always take a little time to allow yourself to become centered and grounded as you experience yourself being surrounded by the unconditionally loving energy of the Universe. Let yourself feel grateful for the information that you will receive to share with others looking for answers.

Remember to start with breathing in from the earth and the sky. You may do this by yourself before the session, or you can do this as part of the beginning of the session. Even better, you can do it at both times.

You may thank the Universe and your angels and guides for showing you only the right images when you connect to the spirit world. You may thank the Universe and your team for sending the right spirits that will provide the right information at that time. You may be grateful that you will always maintain an awareness of your conscious world as you open to the messages and information from the Other Side. You may always know that you may end a mediumship session at any time for any reason and return to full consciousness.

TALKING TO ANGELS AND SPIRIT GUIDES

Besides contacting dead people and other spirits, mediums may also be able to identify and communicate with the angels or spirit guides of the people for whom they do readings. These entities appear to the medium in the same way he or she would experience any other communication from the Other Side. The angels or spirit guides may be seen, heard, felt, smelled, or tasted, or the medium simply may have a knowing.

It is also possible that a medium's own spirit guide or an angel is actually providing the information during the spirit communication. In this case, the medium talks to the angel or guide, who then communicates either with the subject's guide(s) or angel(s) or with a loved one on the Other Side. This process may sound complicated, but it really isn't. After sending the message, the medium just waits until the answer comes back. This method is very similar to just knowing, and that knowing may come from a spirit guide or an angel.

Many people would love to know if they have spirit guides or angels. They may have been trying to make contact on their own by creating altered states of consciousness, hoping to make visual contact or hear a voice that can guide them. Just having a medium identify the presence of an angel or spirit guide can help people feel that they are not alone in their journey.

How will you know if it's a spirit guide or an angel when you make contact with energy? First, you may just ask to connect with the subject's spirit guide or angel. The more you practice, the more confident you will become and the more you will learn to trust what you are experiencing. One reason to practice with a group is so that you can compare your results to those of other readers. It is also a good idea to have an experienced instructor give you some pointers when you are beginning to develop your mediumship skills.

You may find that if you see angels or spirit guides, they will appear in the same location around the subjects that you are reading. Many mediums use a spirit's position behind a subject to identify their relationship. For instance, a parent will be in a different location than a grandparent or a sibling. Every experience you have is constantly teaching you how to use your mediumship skills. You may want to make notes about your experiences.

You may find that you communicate with the Other Side through spirit guides or angels rather than directly with deceased loved ones. You may also connect with deceased pets that have messages for their owners or be able to identify the subject's power animal, another type of spirit guide. As you continue your psychic/mediumship development, just be mindful of the different types of communications from the Other Side that you may receive.

EXPLORING MEDIUMSHIP

It's time to try a mediumship exercise to see how you may connect to the Other Side. You have already identified how your mind accepts images through your five different senses of sight, hearing, touch, taste, and smell. You may receive your information through one or as many as all five of them. It is possible that you may not be a natural medium. If that is the case, you have other psychic abilities that you may discover as you continue to do the exercises in this book.

It is recommended that you work with one or more other people when you practice mediumship exercises. You will want to have a subject that the rest of you can practice on. You can take turns being the subject and the reader. The more people you have participating, the more experiences you can compare.

Exercise: Mediumship Practice

The first step is getting centered. Take a few moments away from the hustle and bustle of your daily life to connect to the peaceful, unconditionally loving energy of the Universe flowing over and around you. Your time to become centered may vary in length according to what else is taking place around you. Even one breath of gratitude and Universal Love can help you focus.

As you feel yourself becoming centered and grounded, thank your Source for bringing the right spirits through for you to connect with during the readings. You may thank your Source that your abilities will open and develop to be used for the greater good of both the person being read and the spirits coming through. It is okay to be nervous and wonder if what you are getting is just your imagination. Remember that imagination has to come from someplace, so be open to whatever comes through.

You may ask that you only receive information that is going to be positive for the subject. It is advisable not to tell subjects directly that you see a negative event in their life in the future, such as death. Instead, you may suggest that they may want to avoid an area, an activity, or perhaps have a medical checkup. After all, the future is always open to change.

Once you get together to practice with one or more others, take another brief moment, either together or by yourselves, to reinforce your centering as you enter an altered state of focus, ready to begin. If there are more than two of you, start by focusing your attention on one person. You may have this person sit or stand apart from the others, perhaps in a centralized location.

Concentrate your gaze just off to the side of the subject so that you are not looking directly at him or her. Now let your eyes go out of focus like looking at a holographic picture that contains two different views.

* If you are visual, what do you see? Can you see images around the subject? If you do, what are you seeing? Can you see physical forms? Where are they in relation to the subject? Are they on the right, on the left, or above her?

* If you are seeing people, do you relate any of them to relationships in your life? If you are experiencing an image like this, it

may be giving you a clue about someone coming through who has the same relationship with the subject. If you see someone on your mother's side, the same would be true for the subject. You may be directly seeing the subject's relatives, and as you practice, you will find a consistency between the location where you see the images and how they connect to the subject's family.

* You may actually see scenes playing out in front of you of important events that took place during the deceased's lifetime. You may see symbols that help you interpret the meaning of the message that the spirit is trying to communicate to the subject.

* Are you getting sound images? Do you hear or feel that someone on the Other Side is trying to speak to you or send a message through you? If you do, either make note of it if you are in a group, or if you are the only one doing the reading, tell the subject directly.

* Are you getting any feelings, either emotionally or physically? If so, how do they relate to the person who has passed?

* Finally, are you receiving smells or tastes, and, if so, how do they relate to the communication?

When you have finished this exercise, compare with other participants what you have experienced. Now get feedback from the subject. You may find that some get different images than you while others may get something similar. Each one of you will experience mediumship differently. Just like developing any skill, it is a combination of using your natural ability coupled with the willingness to keep practicing that will help you become a medium and may help many others along your life path.

GIVE A READING

Are you ready to start doing mediumship readings? Actually, if you have been practicing the exercise in the last section, you have already started. You may find that there are classes being offered in your area that will help you work with an organized group. Most Spiritualist churches offer mediumship courses and even certifications when you have reached a certain level of proficiency. If that is not an option, you might put your own group together to practice.

There comes a point when it is time to try your mediumship skills on people who you do not know. You can give a reading either to individuals or to a group. Usually an individual appointment is for a specific time period. It could be a half-hour to an hour. The longer the appointment, the deeper you have a chance to go. You may want to record the reading or have the subject record it, as well as have someone take notes. When the information is flowing, it is very easy to forget some of the details that are being passed along.

You may just read for a subject without any dialogue between you for part of the session. Some mediums just talk for a while before they get input from the subject. Others may prefer to have feedback throughout the session. In a group setting, time is always the problem. Don't spend too long with one subject if you are trying to read for everyone in the session, and start with ten or less in a group.

Always remember that you are only as good as your Source. There is no need to have an ego when it comes to being a medium. There are many "legends in their own minds" who think they are good. The good ones are just plain everyday people with extraordinary gifts.

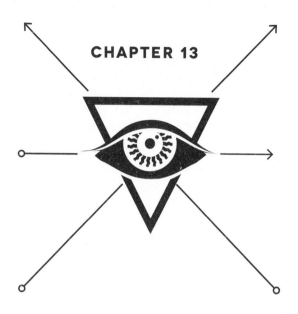

CHAPTER 13

HOW TO INVESTIGATE GHOSTS

Have you ever seen, heard, or felt a ghost? In this chapter, you will consider how your psychic abilities can help you investigate ghosts. Believe it or not, you can use an altered state of consciousness to help amplify connections to the unseen. You will learn about ghosts and where they haunt, how to go about exploring a haunted house, and what equipment can help verify what you psychically uncover. Finally, you will have a chance to try out your animal communication skills by reading a photograph of an animal that has passed over and attempting to contact the animal.

CONTACT WITH GHOSTS

Have you ever felt the hair stand up on the back of your head? Perhaps you have felt a sudden temperature drop or experienced a cold chill, followed by the feeling that something abnormal was happening around you. All of these experiences may possibly be called "paranormal experiences," indicating that you may have connected to the world of the unseen. They sometimes happen and disappear so quickly that it is easy to dismiss what has just happened as your imagination. Perhaps as you read this chapter, you will find that you have had ghostly encounters your whole life without accepting them as real.

The residual energy matter of a deceased person or animal—what we call a ghost—can manifest itself in several ways and is experienced through our five different senses. It is possible to see, hear, feel, smell, or perhaps experience tastes connected to ghosts. If you are sensitive in one or more of your senses, you may pick up more ghost energy than people with less sensitivity.

Children usually have more encounters with spirits than adults. They are open and act as a beacon, drawing the ghosts to them. As people get older, they usually learn how to create boundaries that keep spirits at a distance. Can you remember any experiences you had when you were a child that could be attributed to a haunting?

Have you ever seen what you thought to be a ghost? If so, how would you describe it? Was it solid—that is, could you make out its shape, or was it just a shadow? Have you ever caught a movement out of the corner of your eye that disappeared when you tried to focus on it? How often and how many times have you had visual ghost encounters in your life?

Have you ever heard sounds or voices when there was no one around to create them? Have you ever heard music or other sounds that could not rationally be explained? If so, how many times in your life has this phenomenon occurred? Have you ever felt the presence of a ghost or a spirit, such as a loved one or even a pet that has passed over and perhaps comes back to visit?

Maybe you have experienced a ghost who is very negative. Have you ever felt physical sensations, such as a push or shove that you couldn't explain? Some people have even felt themselves being scratched by something unseen that actually left a physical mark on their body. Have you ever witnessed strange movements, such as doors opening and shutting? How many of these experiences have you had during your life? Was there a specific place or a time when heightened activity was taking place around you?

All of these questions are designed to remind you of how you may have already been having contact with ghosts throughout your life. You may have even had an "imaginary" friend as a child that you thought was real. Guess what? Your imaginary friend may have just been a real ghost. Unfortunately, it is well-meaning adults who often close the door to the spirit world for children by telling them they are just imagining and cautioning them not to talk about what they see.

WHAT ARE GHOSTS?

Ghosts seem to exist almost everywhere that people do. But what exactly is a ghost? A ghost is a spirit that exists near the earth plane. The spirit may be trapped in a world between worlds for one or more reasons. It may have had its human life ended suddenly and possibly tragically, and the soul unexpectedly found itself separated from its body. It could not get back in and didn't know where to go next, thus finding itself suspended in a timeless environment. Some ghosts are not ready to move on because they died with unfinished business that keeps them connected to the earth plane.

The typical concept of a haunted house is an old building with a lot of history. Maybe it's a dilapidated structure that sits in silence, its occupants long since gone. This picture in our minds makes a great backdrop for a horror movie but is far from a typical haunted house. Yet the more history a house has, the more opportunity there is for spirits to exist.

Can Ghosts Communicate?

Do ghosts have intelligence and the ability to communicate with people? The answer seems to be that some spirits do have these abilities. For instance, a ghost that lived and perhaps died in a house that he or she owned while alive may still have a strong connection to it as a spirit. You have probably heard stories of someone moving into an old house and then attempting to make changes. That's when some ghosts make their presence known.

Pieces of jewelry are popular items for ghosts to "borrow." If you are having possessions mysteriously disappear, just ask the ghost to please bring them back. They should reappear just as mysteriously.

Perhaps there is more than one ghost, and the spirits themselves do not get along. Their personal battle can often affect the house's occupants on a psychological level, creating conflict for everyone occupying the space.

Spirits can resent someone coming into "their house" and taking it over. Tools and other objects can disappear. Things can be rearranged when no one's there. If someone in the house is worried, the spirit may react to what is going on by scattering items about. On the other hand, a ghost may welcome a new family and keep a protective watch over the occupants.

Some ghosts seem to watch after children. There are many stories of children being rescued from precarious positions by an unseen force, or toys mysteriously materializing for a child to play with. Teenagers may find that their CDs or iPods can disappear when they are being played too loud.

Where Do Ghosts Come From?

Believe it or not, you could live in a new house that has a ghost. Ghosts not only come with houses, but they also come with the land or with belongings. You may have an antique that is haunted. You may or may not have been related to the spirits that are connected to the things in your home.

Ghosts of deceased family members may choose to live close by to loved ones still on this side. Sometimes they will exist around one family for a period of time and then move on to another relative in a different location.

Ghosts may have a strong connection to a specific location and be very protective of that place. Some ghosts continue to haunt the same location, playing out the same scene over and over again. Usually this type of haunt is connected to a traumatic event that left an imprint on the location.

DEVELOP YOUR GHOST-HUNTING SKILLS

There are two points of view held by ghost hunters regarding how to go about exploring haunted houses. One faction wants to collect verifiable evidence only with traditional equipment, and the other wants to use psychic help along with tools. The goal of this section is to help show you how to develop your own ghost-hunting skills in conjunction with collecting hard evidence. Remember, others may not accept what you pick up psychically unless there is also physical proof of a ghost encounter.

You may want to put together a team of paranormal investigators or join an existing team. It is not recommended that you investigate a haunted house by yourself. In fact, it may be a good idea to team up at first with someone who has had prior ghost-hunting experience.

As most haunted house investigations take place at night, it is very possible to run into safety hazards. It is also possible to run into the unexpected when dealing with the spirit world. Ghostly experiences can happen suddenly and without warning, especially if the spirit does not want you there.

You may have a specific house in mind to explore, or you may want to investigate a site that has a haunted reputation. Whatever the case, make sure you have permission from the owners. Cemeteries are popular spots for many ghost hunters, but again, always have permission to be in or around the premises.

Get Prepared

Do your research on any haunted house you hope to investigate. Interview anyone who may have lived there or may have had a paranormal experience at that location. Learn the history of the property, including who the previous owners were and what took place on the land before it had a building. Check out rumors or old stories about the property. Historical societies, libraries, and old newspaper accounts may all provide clues to what may be haunting the property.

Finally, be prepared for the unexpected. Just as you would do for a mediumship reading, take some time to prepare for the investigation by getting "centered." If you are working with others, you may want to have a group meditation before you begin. If you run into negative energy, don't try to challenge it. There are professionals, such as members of the clergy, who specialize in dealing with demons and performing exorcisms. Remember that ghost hunting and exploring haunted houses is not just fun and games. When you investigate a haunted house, you are stepping into an unseen world that is as real as the world you live in.

Ghost-Hunting Tools

Traditional ghost hunters or paranormal investigators use several items to assist them when they investigate a haunted house. Some established teams have several thousand dollars' worth of equipment at their disposal. You can start your journey on a shoestring budget with material you may already have, including:

* Notepad and something to write with

* Flashlight

* Extra clothes in case it gets cold during the watch

* Tape measure to keep a record of distances

* Pendulum and/or L-rods (These dowsing tools can not only locate water but they can also find electromagnetic energy that may be generated by a ghost.)

* Digital camera to capture spirit orbs

* Camcorder or video camera to record in places that may have a lot of spirit activity

* Digital voice recorder that you can use with audio editing software, such as Audacity, to help you analyze the results of your search

If you want to invest more money in ghost-hunting tools, you may want to purchase an EMF meter to help measure electromagnetic fields. Another useful electronic tool is an infrared thermometer to measure temperature fluctuations that can indicate a ghost is in your presence. You can find many other tools by researching ghost-hunting websites, and there are also new products being developed all the time.

DOCUMENT AND RECORD EVERYTHING

There are always going to be skeptics when it comes to proving that there really are spirits or ghosts. It doesn't matter whether the information is collected psychically or by using electronic equipment. When presenting evidence or findings, you may want to let each person make up his own mind rather than trying to prove the absolute validity of the evidence you have gathered. Until more sophisticated ghost-tracking equipment is developed, chances are there will always be questions connected to any evidence gathered.

Remember, you are a guest in the spirit world when you are investigating the paranormal. Respect the environment you are entering. The more you investigate and learn of the unseen world that exists around you, the more you will learn to develop and use your psychic abilities.

An interesting way to gather evidence in a haunted house is to work with a subject in a trance state. It may be possible to establish direct communication with a ghost through the unconscious mind. It is best that a professionally trained hypnotist or someone with equal expertise in the field of ghost and spirit communication facilitate this type of session. A good subject can easily enter into a deep altered state of consciousness.

Once the subject is in a deep altered state of consciousness, the facilitator can ask questions that help identify any spirit energy that is present. To rule out outside influences, the subject should not be familiar with the history of the location. Record all the action from the very beginning until the end. If you edit the results, make sure you retain an uncut and unedited copy of the original in your files.

If you are using a psychic to locate and communicate with ghosts, it is also a good idea to record everything. If the psychic gets information that leads to a contact, having the electronic evidence to back up what happened during the investigation can help build a case for an actual haunting. Video is better than just audio, but the more perspectives of the same situation you can collect, the better the results may be. Video should also be used to corroborate the activity of devices such as EMF meters.

If you have more than one psychic on an investigation, compare the impressions that each one received. What information did they get that was the same, and what did they get that was different? One psychic may perceive visual images, while another may feel the ghost's mood.

Finally, take your time in putting the evidence together after you have finished your investigation. It takes a lot of patience to put together an investigation, and it may require more than one visit. Then it can require many more hours to go through all the material you have collected. Keep in mind that the one-hour ghost-hunting shows on television can actually take more than a week of investigation, and then all that evidence must be analyzed.

COMMUNICATING WITH ANIMALS

Many people have a natural psychic ability to communicate with animals. The interesting thing is that most of the people who can do this do not recognize that they are animal communicators. The truth is that many people are closer to animals than they are to people. A pet usually accepts its owner with unconditional love. The owner's response for the animal is likewise.

The animal can read its owner's moods, and the owner can usually read what's going on with the animal. Together they often forge a bond that lasts long after the beloved pet has passed on. Animal spirits come back to visit, just as human spirits do. Many pet owners think of their animals as they would a human. The owner may not realize just how large a role their psychic ability has played in their pet communication.

Animal communicator Maia Kincaid, creator of The Animal Listening Project, believes that if all people who own animals would listen to them, there would be no need for animal shelters. Imagine how the care of animals would improve if people could understand why an animal behaves the way it does or what it feels physically and mentally.

How Do You Read an Animal?

You read an animal in just the same way as you would read a human, only the animal can't give you verbal feedback. You receive your information through your five senses; you may get your animal information through your visual sense, your hearing sense, your kinesthetic sense, your tasting sense, your smelling sense, or in combinations of any or all of these. Usually the communication between human and animal is nonverbal, simply mind to mind.

If you have one or more animals, how do you pick up information about them? Take a moment to become centered and open yourself to the unconditionally loving energy of the Universe to help guide you in communicating with animals. If there is an animal available, focus on it for a moment. Can you pick up any visual images connected to it?

Why Would You Read an Animal?

You may see situations in an animal's life that affect it in one way or another. You may see an existing health problem. You may hear the animal in your mind telling you what is going on with it or how it feels about its owner. You may feel how the animal feels, either physically or emotionally. You may get a taste or smell that indicates something about an animal. If the animal has passed, it may send back a message from a person on the Other Side who is there with the animal. Perhaps you can think back over your life and identify times when you were able to communicate with an animal without realizing it.

Animal communication can be especially helpful to owners who have adopted their pets from an animal shelter or rescue association. It is not unusual for adopted animals to have endured some sort of trauma in their life. It could have been abuse or possibly survival from a natural disaster. Just knowing what is going on with an animal could be a huge help in assisting its adjustment to its new living conditions. Perhaps you have a talent at communicating with animals that can be of great service to the animal and its owner alike.

Exercise: Read an Animal's Photograph

Many animal communicators do not need an animal present to give a psychic reading. They often can get all the information they need from a picture of the animal that has passed over. By reading a photograph, an animal communicator can work with a client anywhere on earth. Of course, this method can also work for doing readings on people as well. Remember, Cayce would do accurate readings from requests received by mail, and he didn't even have a photo of the subject.

Let's see how well you do at reading an animal's photograph. First, you need to have one or more photos that you can practice with. It is a good idea to start with reading animals whose owners can give you feedback. Through the use of the Internet, you are not limited to someone in your area, and you do not have to wait for a photo to be sent through regular mail. Make sure that you receive a clear image of the animal for the reading.

To read an animal's photograph, you will want to use the imagery techniques that you have developed in earlier chapters.

Start by getting centered. Allow the unconditionally loving energy of the Universe to flow through and balance your chakras.

As you breathe in this energy, open yourself to your team that works with you and guides you through your psychic imagery process. When you feel balanced and in tune, turn your attention to the animal photo you have selected. Let your eyes go slightly out of focus as you open yourself to the images that the animal shows you.

Do you see any images around the animal? If so, what do they show or tell you? Perhaps you are seeing scenes from the animal's life that may have had an effect on it. Maybe you are seeing auras or colors that may give an indication of its health. Perhaps you can actually scan its body and see inside for any issues. What else can you see relating to the photo?

Can you hear the animal speaking to you if you ask it a question? Perhaps you are hearing the voice of your guide or angel feeding you information about the animal. You may ask a question relating to the animal and receive the answer back as your own voice or just as a knowing that you can verbalize. Are there any other sound images that you receive from the photo?

Do you get any feelings from the photo? You may feel how the animal feels, either physically or emotionally. You may get an understanding of how the animal feels about its surroundings or its owners. You may imagine that you are placing your hands on or over its body and getting a reading about its physical condition. What other sensations do you pick up through your kinesthetic sense when you read the photo?

Can you pick up any smells or tastes related to the animal? If so, what are they telling you? Perhaps there are people with it who have also passed. What other information did you get from the animal's photograph?

Remember, it's okay to just use your imagination until you gain confidence in what you are picking up from animal photographs. It's just like developing any other natural gift. It is the willingness to put the time into honing your skills that pays off in the long run. You may want to record your voice as you do the readings to help you recall all the information that you receive.

CHAPTER 14

RECEIVE INFORMATION THROUGH DREAMS

Everyone dreams—even though each person's experience is different—but not everyone can remember his or her dreams. If you make a habit of writing down or recording your dreams after you wake up, you may find that you will begin to recognize the various types of dreams that you are having and what they mean to you. Then you will be able to work with the psychic information that you receive while in your dream state.

THE MYSTERY OF DREAMS

Dreams are a great medium for receiving psychic information. They come at a time when your conscious mind is at rest and open to the messages of your unconscious mind and your Universal Mind. Because the conscious mind is so active, many people do not relax enough while awake to tap into the information that is available. At night, you may have many dreams, but most of them go unnoticed. Even if you are aware of having dreamed when you wake up, you may quickly forget the contents of those dreams.

Dream Recall

When you prepare for bed, make an entry into your dream journal—you can also use a digital recorder. Make sure the listing includes the time, what you last ate and when, and how you feel mentally, physically, and spiritually. If you have a request for your guides, angels, higher power, or just for the Universe, ask that an answer may come in your dreams.

When you wake, make sure that you record your dreams as you remember them. Include as many details about your dream as you can remember—the type of dream, theme, people, places, time period, and whether you have had this or similar dreams before.

If you dream of something more than once, pay attention. Many psychic dreams are given to you for a specific reason. They may concern your health, safety, or even career choice.

Just as with any other type of memory, you may remember more of a dream over time. There are many pieces of information that the conscious mind doesn't notice, but they are taken in and stored in the unconscious mind. Your post-dream notes can help prime the pump for your unconscious memory. Once the memory is activated, it is possible to recall a lot more of the dream experience than was first noted.

Dream Patterns

Even if you wake with no conscious memory of a dream, make a note in your journal about how you feel. Over a period of time, the data you collect will help you establish your sleep and dream patterns. Do your dreams occur regularly or sporadically? Do you remember dreams daily, weekly, monthly, or less often than that? Do you have specific dreams for specific moments in your life? Do you dream more when you eat certain foods before you go to bed?

When you first begin to work with your dreams, you may not feel as if you are making a lot of progress. The more patience you have, and the more willing you are to experiment with your dreams, the easier it may be to understand them.

The following sections will help you distinguish between various types of psychic dreams, including dreams that have to do with your past lives, dreams concerning the future, symbolic dreams, dreams of healing and creativity, and dreams that you share with others.

DREAMS OF PAST LIVES

One type of dream that often starts in childhood and may or may not continue into adulthood is a dream that deals with a past life. Children may not recognize that what they are dreaming is from a past life, but they may notice that in their dream, they and their family members appear in different roles.

A past-life dream is set during a different time period. The dream may be repetitious and have a theme that was imprinted in the memory of your soul at the time of the experience. It's not unusual for the past-life dream to be traumatic—many of these dreams are nightmares. For example, a past-life dream may be an event that led up to a death scene, with the dream ending before the actual event. Upon waking, the feeling of terror lingers.

Past-life dreams are often karmic in nature. In other words, your dream may relate to unfinished business from a previous lifetime. The dream may give you a clue as to how you can resolve the karma in your current lifetime. It is possible to use a past-life dream as the catalyst to go deeper into the past life through techniques used by a past-life specialist.

Look for Significant Details or Clues

Here is how you can figure out whether a particular dream is giving you clues or revealing scenes from a past life. Often, these dreams have visual images that you recognize. Does the dream's location seem familiar and yet as though it doesn't belong to your lifetime? Sometimes that distinction is easy to make, and sometimes it is not. A child may not recognize the difference of a few years, whereas an adult would. Also, if the turnaround time between incarnations is short, the child may blend his or her current life with the one that he or she experienced just previously.

If there are people in the dream, how are they dressed? Are they wearing modern clothes? Can you see yourself in the dream, or are you only experiencing it? If you cannot see yourself, hypnosis may help you get more information about who the characters in your dream may have been.

Is there anything else that may give you a clue that you have experienced a past-life dream? You may awake from a past-life dream with an emotion that connects to another lifetime. What other clues would you collect from a dream that would imply it may have been about your past lives?

Dreams of Flight

Past-life dreams can also be experienced as flying dreams. Have you ever dreamed that you are able to soar in the sky, as free as a bird? Some people believe that dreams of flying date back to the earliest reincarnations of your soul, going back to a time when you had no physical form. At that time, you were able to travel using the pure energy of thought as your power. Dreams give your soul a chance to fly again without the constraints of your physical, human body.

Do you fly in any of your dreams? If so, where do you go? Do you travel to other worlds or to heavenly realms? Do you fly backward or forward in time? Where else do you fly? Do you fly alone or with others? Can you choose a destination before you go to sleep and fly there during a dream? Do you ever dream about falling or floating? Is there a pattern to these dreams? It is a good idea to keep track of the answers to these questions by writing them down in a dream journal so you will have something to refer to and make notes in as you track your dreams in the future.

DREAMS OF THE FUTURE

Do you have dreams about events that have not happened yet? This type of dream is called a prophetic dream. Many of the great prophets throughout history relied on their dreams to provide the insights that helped rulers make their decisions about the future. Their predictions could have included floods, famines, and other weather changes. They also may have dreamed of predictions of wars and of threats to the people, the land, and even the rulers themselves.

Some people actually dream so deeply that they leave their body and another entity comes in to occupy it. Before you go to sleep, remind yourself to stay grounded at all times.

When you are out of balance and your energy centers are open, you are susceptible to receiving psychic images from the Universe. These images include events that have not yet happened. When you go to sleep in a state of confusion and imbalance, your dreams may become a conduit for images of the future. Unfortunately, many of these types of dreams are not happy, but tragic.

For example, Jenny, an early-childhood schoolteacher, had a very unsettling dream of a teenage boy being beaten and then a large building blowing up. The images were so strong that she could barely concentrate the next day in school. At home after work, she turned on the television, and there on the screen was the building she had seen in her dreams the night before. It was the Oklahoma City bombing.

Examine Your Prophetic Dreams

Is there a pattern to your prophetic dreams? Do you dream of winning numbers in the lottery before they are drawn? Do you dream about questions and answers on tests before you take them? Do you dream of meeting people and then actually meet them?

Do you dream of future events? If so, are these related to your life and the lives of others you know? Are your dreams about events that may take place on a worldwide scale? Do you dream of disasters before they happen, such as plane crashes, assassinations of famous people, or wars? How often do you have this type of dream?

Prophetic dreams may be messages from your guides, angels, or other forms of higher power. They are often given to you as a warning for the future. Listen to yourself after you have a prophetic dream. Your psychic intuition will indicate how you should respond.

How do you feel during and after a prophetic dream? Do you feel helpless, or are you compelled to take action as a result of your dream? Where do you think your prophetic dreams are coming from? Do you wish that you could block out this type of dream? What else do you experience when you have a dream about the future?

As you make note of your answers to these and other questions in this book, it will help you understand the nature of how your mind works. Remember, if you are so emotionally involved with what you are dreaming, it will be harder to get a clear picture of the psychic information you are receiving. If you can dissociate from your mind's images, you may find that you have a better perspective on your dream experiences.

Alter Your Dreams

It's possible to change a dream's outcome if you enter into a state known as lucid dreaming. Lucid dreaming occurs when a dream continues during the waking state right after you have returned to consciousness. As you become fully aware that you are still experiencing the dream, you have the opportunity to control the dream events and change the dream's outcome. Try entering your dream state again, and consciously change the outcome of the dream. If it is a bad dream, run your positive feelings of peace and love over the negative images and sleep in peace.

SYMBOLIC DREAMS

Once in a while, you will experience a dream that feels like a riddle. It may involve snippets and pieces of events in your life, usually close in time to when the dream is experienced. These snippets may be from news accounts, or they may come from some memory in your unconscious mind. These events or people you have recently encountered are woven into the dream theme but are out of character with the actual events.

Symbolic dreams may come in sequences or segments. They may be experienced over several different nights or weeks. The dreams can relate to you or to events that are taking place in the world. Dream themes can deal with events that have happened or with events that have yet to happen.

To help you identify a dream that has symbolic content, note the apparent theme of the dream. Is it repeated in the dream? Do you have the same dream or a series of different dreams with the same recurring theme? Are there people, animals, or other beings in your symbolic dreams?

Symbolic dreams are easily dismissed as nonsense dreams. These are dreams that are often attributed to too much rich food or experiences you might have lived through earlier in the day. Even when a dream seems to make no sense, make a note of it in your dream journal, and you may find a pattern developing in your symbolic dreams.

Do you have houses or rooms of a house in your dreams? How do the dreams make you feel? Can you hear voices or other sounds? Do the actions in the dreams make any sense to you at first review? What else can you note from your dreams that may be considered symbolic?

Analysis of a symbolic dream can be complicated due to the subject material and how it relates to you. Try to record as much information as soon as possible in your dream journal. Someone else, or a book on dreams, may provide a clue as to the meaning of your dream and why you dreamed it.

HEALING DREAMS

Healing dreams are not as common as other types of dreams, but they can often occur at times when they are needed. Healing dreams may originate from either the unconscious mind or the Universal Mind. You may be too consciously involved with the medical condition of loved ones or yourself to look at the situation rationally. In other words, you may not hear what you are unconsciously telling yourself.

Dreams are a good way for your unconscious mind to get the message up to your conscious mind. While you are asleep, you are not analyzing the images sent up to you. Valuable clues to your medical condition, and possibly even your treatment, can come from your unconscious mind. The same may be true for information given to you about others, including friends and family. This information may provide you with a different perspective.

A healing dream could also help provide resolutions for old conflicts with friends or family. These dream images may come to you with information that will give you a way to say or write the right words to someone. They may include new insights that will help you resolve, either in your own mind or in communication with others, a situation that needs to be resolved and healed. A healing dream may come in the form of inspiration to compose or create a work of art or a poem that will bring about healing.

Examining Healing Dreams

Do you have healing dreams? If so, how often? Are they dreams about yourself, members of your family, or other people? How do you receive your information—in symbols, actual pictures, voices, feelings, or in some other way? Do you wake up with a feeling of knowing that there is healing, rather than dreaming a picture image?

Do you ask for healing information to come through for you or others before you go to sleep? If so, how often do you get answers? Do you get healing messages to pass on to others? Do you receive healing poems, music, or artistic ideas in your dreams? If so, can you complete the idea into something that helps heal yourself or others?

SHARED DREAMING

A dream experienced simultaneously between two or more people is known as a shared dream. Some shared dreams may be prophetic and signal a world event to come. These dreams may happen within a short time span, often only a few days before the event actually happens. Other shared dreams are simpler—they may be something that you share with a friend. Later, both of you realize that you had the same dream.

Some of the world's great inventions have come from the dream state. Ideas for great books, music, and poetry can come through dreams. They can come from your unconscious mind, usually when you have been thinking about a particular topic or problem. The unconscious mind simply put together all the information it had and sent it up to you while you were in your dream state.

Members of the same family may share past-life dreams as well. These dreams can go unnoticed for years unless someone brings up the subject for discussion. One couple found they both had the same recurring dream of drowning. They eventually discovered that their son had been having the same dream.

Compare Your Dreams

Have you ever discussed your dreams with other family members or friends? If so, have you found any similarities between your dreams and theirs? If you have not brought up the subject of dreams, you may want to try it. Suggest that you and a friend keep dream journals and compare them. You might like to form a dream group and meet at specific times to discuss your dreams.

The Internet is an excellent way to share your dream experiences. There are many websites dedicated to dream sharing and interpretation. You may be surprised to discover when you begin to talk about dreams with friends or family members that you have been dreaming the same thing for quite a while.

REVIEWING YOUR DREAMS

When you first begin to work with your dreams, be patient with yourself. It may take a while for you to develop your dream recall technique. The way you recall is different from anyone else, and so is the psychic information you receive in your dreams. It's like learning any other skill; the more you practice, the more you will learn to recall and interpret what you are experiencing through your dreams. Your dreams are truly the mirror image of your soul.

It is not uncommon for you to have a visit from a deceased friend or relative in your dreams. They may come to you to comfort or warn you. The same thing may happen with your angels or guides. Your inner guidance system continues to work when you are asleep.

You can use relaxation exercises to help you review your dreams. Before you let yourself go into a trance, reread or listen to your notes on the dream sequence that you want to review. Keep these handy so that you can refer to them again when you are in a relaxed state. When you're ready, get comfortable. Focus on your breathing and begin to relax your body.

Exercise: Examine Your Dreams

Let your eyes close, and take a few comfortable breaths. You may feel the Universal Flow of peaceful, unconditionally loving energy over and around your body as you sense all your chakras opening and balancing. You may suggest to yourself that when you want to refer to your notes, you may open your eyes and still feel very relaxed and able to recall the memories of your dream. When you're ready, let the images of a part of your dream come into focus. You may experience your images in all five senses: by seeing, hearing, feeling, tasting, and smelling.

If you are visual, focus on the images in your mind and see if you can change your view, bringing images closer or moving them back. Try to stop the action so that you can look for things you missed before. Now try to imagine the sounds that go with the images. If you can, change the volume or move around in the image and hear sounds as you move. Next, add feeling to your images.

Can you experience emotions connected to your dream? Can you place yourself in the dream and experience textures, temperatures, tastes, and smells? Can you experience your dream in all the five different senses? Can you discover things in your dream that you had not noticed before? Can you back up the dream to a point earlier than you can remember, or can you move forward to continue the dream beyond where it had stopped?

IMPROVING YOUR PSYCHIC DREAMING

If you are an active dreamer, or if you feel that your dreams can be a good resource for providing you with information from either your unconscious mind or your Universal Mind, here is an exercise to help you tune in to your dreams even better.

Exercise: Ask for Dream Information

One of the most important things to do before going to sleep is to make sure you are grounded, in balance with your energy centers, and in tune with your Belief and your internal and external guidance systems. If you create an anchor to put yourself in touch with your guidance systems, you will be able to enter that state before you fall asleep.

Once you've done this, take a deep breath, focus on your third eye, and feel Universal peace and love flowing through you. Even though you may not want to, or you have trouble experiencing these feelings, remember that they are not related to whatever else is taking place in your life. They are just simple relaxing waves of energy provided by the Universe.

At this time, ask your Belief or your guides, angels, or other beings for help with your worries and anxieties. Ask that the information you receive from your dreams be the right information for what is needed at this particular moment.

CHAPTER 15

THE ART OF DOWSING

Most people think dowsing is the act of searching for water or minerals hidden in the earth by relying on a dowsing rod. However, psychic dowsing may be used in many aspects of your life, as you will learn in this chapter. Various forms of psychic dowsing may be performed with a pendulum, Y-rods, L-rods, a bobber, and even your fingers.

WHAT IS DOWSING?

Dowsing is the ancient art of gathering information with the use of dowsing tools. There are historical records that indicate that dowsers have been around since the times of ancient Egypt and China. The best-known tools are the pendulum, the forked stick, and the Y-rods, but there are several others as well. The Europeans used dowsers during the Middle Ages to locate underground supplies of coal. There is no scientific explanation as to why dowsing works. It is thought to be an extension of psychic ability.

Today most people associate dowsing with hunting for water. The ancient name "water witch" or "water wizard" is often still applied to someone who has a talent for dowsing for water. However, there is a lot more to dowsing than just finding water. Many psychics use the art of dowsing to help them enhance their abilities. It can be used for locating oil, deposits of other rich minerals—even lost people!

Dowsers played a very important role in the Vietnam War. They were used to search for and find land mines. The ancient art of dowsing was regarded by some as more accurate than modern mine-detecting technology.

Dowsing can involve the different senses, especially the "feeling" and visual senses. Most dowsers say that they simply "get a feeling" that helps them make decisions. Others allow their feelings to create a visual image, or an image using other senses. Learning the art of dowsing is like learning to play a musical instrument. The more you practice and learn your strengths, the more you will define your abilities.

PREPARE YOURSELF BEFORE DOWSING

Just as with other psychic modalities, it is advisable for you always to take the time to center yourself before beginning to dowse. Once you are comfortable getting yourself centered, anchor the feeling so that you may recall it whenever you want to dowse.

Take a deep breath and slowly exhale. You can do this anywhere you are, standing or sitting. Now focus for a moment on your third eye, and feel yourself connecting to your Universal Mind. With your next breath, inhale the unconditional love and peace of the Universe. Allow yourself to be open to the psychic flow that guides your ability to dowse.

Now you are ready to start dowsing. Practice by focusing on the Universe's energy flowing over and around you as your chakras open and come into balance. Focus and release; repeat the process a few times. Once you get used to focusing on your third eye, you will find that this will actually help center you.

DOWSING WITH A PENDULUM

The pendulum is the easiest method of dowsing to learn; the term itself is a fancy word for any object suspended from a string or chain so that you can swing it freely. It should have some weight to it, but you don't want a pendulum that's either too heavy or too light. The weight can be of any material, from a fine crystal to a metal washer. The length of the chain or string can be up to a foot long.

You don't need to make your own pendulum from scratch—a necklace with a stone or pendant would do just fine, as long as it will dangle freely and comfortably from your fingers. An old-fashioned pocket watch can also be used for dowsing.

Getting Started

Many people make daily decisions with the help of their pendulums, through the responses they receive from how the pendulum swings. Using a dowsing pendulum is another way for keeping in touch with your inner guides, your unconscious, and the Universal Mind.

When you have found the right implement and have centered yourself, take hold of the string with your thumb and first finger. If holding it that way is a problem, you can try bracing it with your other hand, holding your forearm just below the elbow. You can also rest your pendulum arm on a support. Let the pendulum swing freely, eight inches to a foot below your thumb and finger. Now hold the pendulum in front of you, with your thumb and finger at eye level and at a comfortable distance away from your head, approximately eighteen inches.

Show Me "Yes"

First, you'll want to figure out which movement of the pendulum will indicate a positive answer. Let the pendulum dangle freely for a moment. Keep your two eyes focused on the hanging part, and open your mind to be guided by your team. When you are ready, ask the pendulum, "Show me 'yes.'" The pendulum will swing in one direction. Keep your arm as steady as possible and let the pendulum go to work. It may swing back and forth, sideways, or front to back, or it may rotate in a circle either clockwise or counterclockwise. Let it swing freely for a few moments until you can clearly see what direction the pendulum swings to indicate "yes."

Show Me "No"

Now that you have established the direction of "yes," ask the pendulum to show the direction of "no." Again, make sure that you are allowing the pendulum to swing freely, and pay attention to how it changes direction to indicate "no." Now ask it to reaffirm "yes" again, and watch as it changes direction again. You can practice changing between "yes" and "no" several times so that you will get used to the different ways the pendulum swings.

Now ask the pendulum to stop, and wait until it comes to a standstill. Your pendulum should slowly stop its swinging. As you practice, this exercise will relax you, allowing your mind to open to your inner guidance while you focus on the pendulum with your eyes.

Ask for Permission

Now you are ready to ask your pendulum questions. All questions need to be phrased so that the answers are either a "yes" or a "no." If the pendulum cannot answer the question—if, for instance, the answer is not available—it will come to a standstill.

First, ask your pendulum for permission to ask questions at this time. If it swings in the direction of "yes," you are free to ask questions directed to the source that controls the pendulum. If it is "no," you may not be totally centered or the subject matter may not be appropriate at this time.

Ask Questions

You might start with something simple, like a question about the weather: Will the weather be fair tomorrow? Try something that is relatively unimportant and at the same time can be checked for accuracy. Here are a few other ideas:

* Will the stock market go up today?

* Will I hear from my friend today?

* Will I get a response for a question I've asked today?

Many pendulum users ask questions that they would pose to their guides, angels, or the Universal Mind. They are usually looking for some sort of direction to take when making a decision. These decisions can be as simple as where to eat or as complex as guidance in career moves and relationship situations. Some people involve dowsing in every decision-making aspect of their lives. It is their way of consulting their Belief System.

What Controls the Pendulum?

So who or what is really controlling the pendulum? Is it you, your unconscious mind, or your Universal Mind? Maybe the communication comes from your guides or angels? Or is it purely by random or involuntary body movement related to your questions so that you are giving yourself the answer you want? No one knows for sure.

You will have to decide for yourself as you continue to experiment with dowsing. However, it does seem that there is a strong connection between dowsing and psychic ability. It may become a very important psychic tool for you. Don't get discouraged if your results aren't earth shattering at first. If you find it enjoyable and positive, you can always pick up a dowsing tool when you want to ask for a little more help from the Universe.

FORKED-STICK DOWSING

Using the forked stick, also called the Y-rod, is the most popular and best-known method for water dowsing. The material does not have to be made of wood, although many an old dowser uses a fresh twig cut from an apple or willow tree. The Y-rod can be made from a coat hanger or even plastic wire. The only requirement is that the tool be stiff enough to hold its shape and flexible enough to bend.

> Remember that other dowsing implements are meant as guidance tools for your decision-making process. For major changes, always make sure you have a system of checks and balances so that you are not relying entirely on your dowsing information. Work with your guides, your Belief, and your common sense.

If you are cutting a branch, choose one that can be pruned to a Y shape. Leave two to three inches on the stock end before the Y forks. The length of the Y's branches should be between one and two feet in length. The size and flexibility of the branch may determine the length to which you cut it. Trim off all the "nubs" on the branch that may interfere with holding the stick.

To find your correct dowsing position, bring your upper arms and elbows in, close to the sides of your body, with your forearms bent slightly upward. The palms of your hands should face upward, with your fingers clasping the ends of the Y-rod and your thumbs pointing outward beyond the ends of the rod. Grip the ends tightly in the palms of your hands. The shorter the handles of the Y-rod, the closer your hands need to be.

Pull the rod handles apart until the entire rod, including the point, is parallel to the ground. You are now ready to dowse. The Y-rod may not be as easy for you to work with as the pendulum, so remember to be patient. As you move closer or over a target, the tip of your dowsing rod will begin to pull downward. The closer you get, the more you will feel the pull.

Exercise: Dowse for Water

The best way to test your ability in using a Y-rod is to look for water. Try it over a sink or a known water pipe. Don't hold the rod over the water at first. Make a slow swing until you are in the direction of the water. You should feel a pull. Now move over the source and see if the tip of the rod is pulled downward.

The feeling of the energy that the Y-rod picks up is like an underwater current. This current pulls and bends the rod. Practice dowsing different known water sites, both inside and outside your house or apartment. The more you work with your Y-rod, the more comfortable and confident you will be in your dowsing abilities.

Then, move on to places where the source of water remains unknown—in your backyard, a vacant lot, or out in the country. Ask your Y-rod to locate the best vein of water. Slowly turn in a circle until you feel a pull. Follow the direction of the pull until you are directly over the water supply.

Find the Details

Ask the rod to tell you how deep the water is. Hold it in position and count slowly upward from one. Eventually, you will reach a number when the rod tip is pulled downward. You might want to start in increments of ten feet, such as, "Is the water ten, twenty, thirty, forty feet below ground?" Once you have determined the depth within a ten-foot range, you can go to single feet.

Next, ask the rod how many gallons a minute the water flows. Again, count slowly from one to the number at which you get the greatest pull on your rod. This should give you the speed of the water flow. It is always fun to try this exercise with more than one person and then compare notes after you have finished.

Exercise: Map Dowsing

Believe it or not, you don't have to go to a site in person. You can dowse for water from a map of the property. To try map dowsing, have someone draw a map of his property, leaving out the locations of the water and septic systems. Hold the rod over the map and ask where the water supply is located. Mark where the rod indicates it is.

Try the same for the septic system. If you have more than one person involved, you can compare the results of your dowsing. You can use this method for many other uses as well—for instance, to search for missing people or animals. You can also ask your Y-rod to locate lost items.

Over the years, map dowsers have been employed to locate oil, gold, and uranium deposits using geological maps. A good dowser can hone in on the goal from many miles away.

DOWSING WITH L-RODS

Another method of dowsing uses L-rods. L-rods are usually made of metal, with the most popular made from a bronze welding rod cut in approximately two-foot lengths. The rod is bent at a right angle about four inches from one end. Often, a cardboard or plastic tube is placed over the short end, and the tip is bent again to keep the tube in place.

To hold an L-rod, grip the device by closing your hand around the bent part or handle of the rod vertically, allowing the long part to be able to horizontally swing freely above the hand. If there is no tube covering the handle of the rod, you will need to relax your grip so it can rotate when dowsing. Your arms can find a comfortable outstretched position where the L-rods are able to swing without hitting each other.

You can use either one or two rods, depending on what you seek to uncover when dowsing. One L-rod can be used to establish a direction or for "yes" and "no" answers. Two L-rods are often used to measure energy fields or auras. The tips of the rods can be pushed apart when the energy is encountered or come together when a specific location is desired. Sometimes, the rods are lightly tapped against each other before each dowsing experiment so that they can be cleared of the past energy.

L-rods have traditionally been used to locate underground water and sewer pipes. The dowser starts with the rod tips pointing away, and when the pipe is located, the rod tips cross. You can make L-rods from metal coat hangers. You can also ask "yes" or "no" questions of L-rods in the same way you would with Y-rods.

L-Rods for Measuring Auras

L-rods are great instruments to use for measuring auras. Your body has an energy field that extends a distance out from you. Some of you may have very small auras, which may mean you are open to having your space invaded. If that is the case, the L-rod won't open until it's very close to you. If you have a strong aura, you can spin the L-rod from several feet away from your body.

To measure someone's aura, start from a distance of approximately ten feet, making sure that no one else is in your subject's energy field. Begin to walk slowly toward him, with the L-rod tips facing each other. As you get closer, note the point where the rods swing open. That is the point at which you have entered the person's aura field. Even ten feet may not be far enough away for some people, and if the rods are already open, you may have to step backward until you step outside of the aura.

It is educational and fun to work with several people when you practice your skills at measuring auras. You may also be able to see the auras you are measuring. They may look like colorless waves of energy, or you may see the auras in color. If the L-rod responds well to you, you may have the ability to measure changes in people relating to their attitudes, health, and their positive or negative spiritual growth. You may be able to help many others if you have the gift of working with and changing someone else's aura.

DOWSING WITH A BOBBER

A bobber is another dosing tool; it can be made of different materials, including a wooden twig, a flexible metal rod, or even a piece of plastic. The device can also be made from coiled wire. For the tool to work, there needs to be a weight at the end.

Whatever you use, the bobber must be flexible enough to respond easily to your questions. The length and size can vary from eighteen inches down to a very small device. A spring on the end ensures that there will be a lot of play in the bobber.

To grip a bobber dowsing rod, hold it in the palm of your hand with your thumb on top and pointing away from you. Your forearm should be level, which will mean the bobber rises slightly toward the tip. The bobber on the other end will either bob up and down or sideways. Ask it to show you which way "yes" is, and then where "no" is. Once you have determined "yes" and "no," you are ready to ask your questions.

FINGER AND BODY DOWSING

If you find that you have a natural gift for dowsing, you may not need to have a tool other than your fingers. This ability is part of your mental makeup. Each of you will respond a little differently whether you dowse with a tool or with your fingers. Some of you may feel tingling, heat, cold, or heaviness. You may even have a response through one of your other senses when you use your fingers to dowse.

It is always important to make sure you are centered, grounded, and protected before you begin to dowse with a part of your body. To use your fingers effectively for dowsing, the energy must flow and circulate freely through all of them. Rub your hands together to raise your temperature and get the blood moving. Next, shake your fingers to make sure that you have released any energy that has been absorbed by other fields. Ask your Universal Mind to show you how you will receive accurate information through your fingers that can be used positively to help yourself and others.

If you are dowsing an aura, hold your hand open, with the palms facing the person you are measuring. You may start about two feet away and slowly move closer. As you move in, you should begin to have some sensation in your fingers. You are now feeling the other person's energy field.

As you develop and fine-tune your dowsing abilities, pay close attention to all the information you are receiving. Are you getting images in pictures, sounds in your head, tastes in your mouth, or aromas? If so, these may become very useful as you further develop your psychic gifts.

Remote Finger Dowsing

You can use your fingers in the same way as other dowsing tools to get information from maps or other items. Remember always to ask for specific information. The clearer you are about what it is you are asking for, the more accurate the information that comes back will be. Always start with a large area or general information and then begin to hone in on the target. Check from several different directions.

You can also dowse items such as clothes from a missing person. You can ask for "yes" and "no" sensations through your fingers or other parts of your body and get the same response that a dowsing tool would give you. Your entire body is a resource ready and waiting to assist you in reaching your psychic potential. The more you are aware of your feelings, the more you will begin to know your special gifts.

Body Dowsing

Another popular form of dowsing is body dowsing. To try this, stand up straight and ask a question of yourself for advice or guidance. Phrase it so it can be answered "yes" or "no." Your body may be pulled forward for a "yes" or pushed backward for a "no."

Muscle testing is very similar to body dowsing. One technique is to extend an arm out straight with your palm down. Ask a question and have someone push down on your arm. If the arm is weak, the answer is "no," and if the arm stays strong, the answer is "yes."

There is another version you can try by touching the points of your thumbs and first fingers together in interlocking circles. Ask a question and try to pull the circle apart. If they remain firmly together, you have a "yes" answer, and if your hands pull apart, it is "no."

CREATE YOUR TECHNIQUE

Now that you have had a chance to experiment with several different dowsing techniques, you can choose what's best for you. Once you have determined whether it's the pendulum, the Y-rods, the L-rods, the bobber rod, or your own fingers, you can search out your best tool.

One option is to find a family heirloom such as a special gold chain that means a lot to you. You can also purchase or make dowsing tools. Rely on your psychic intuition to pick out something that feels right. It is important for you to have something that is comfortable to you and that also gives a strong answer. At the same time, you want to remember that it is not the tool that provides the answers. Those come through your unconscious mind and your Universal Mind. It is also a good idea to find a small dowsing tool that you can easily carry with you at all times. A pendulum fits into your pocket or pocketbook, where another type of rod may not.

Once you've picked out a reliable dowsing tool that responds well to your questions and returns good information on things you are searching for, you can use it to look for other psychic tools. Use your dowsing tool to select a good crystal ball, rune set, or a tarot deck. Take your dowsing implement to a metaphysical shop that sells some of these aids. Let your dowsing tool and your intuition help in the selection. For instance, you can ask your dowsing rod for a "yes" or "no" answer to the question of whether a specific psychic tool is right for you to use.

If you find that dowsing is one of your psychic gifts, the more you use it, the more it will work for you and others in your life.

CHAPTER 16

YOUR PSYCHIC TOOLKIT

To help them access their intuitive abilities, psychics will often use tools such as crystal balls, runes, or brewed tea leaves, just to name a few. You may find certain tools that can help raise your intuitive vibration level, so try them all out, and keep yourself open to receiving psychic information.

IDENTIFYING AND WORKING WITH YOUR PSYCHIC TOOLS

Before you begin to work with a tool, always let your energy balance become in tune with the Universe's unconditional love and peace. Take a few moments to center yourself. Use your anchors that connect you to an altered state of consciousness, and feel the protection of the Universe's energy surrounding and filling you with peace and love. Ask your team of angels and guides to assist you in experiencing something positive from the tool you are working with to help you become more in tune with your life map and soul's purpose.

While you are in a relaxed and connected intuitive state, let yourself open up to both your internal and external guidance systems. Internally, ask that the images may come through one or more of your senses that work best for you. Ask that your external team reaffirm what your internal guidance already knows. Then let yourself be aware of the information that may come to you through the tool you are using.

A psychic tool should have the right feel. Trying to use a tool that is not the right one for you may cause you to become ungrounded. Keep in mind that you may have used one or more of these tools in past lives, and picking it up again may feel like second nature to you. You may come across an implement that feels as comfortable as an old shoe. The next step is learning to trust it once more. Once you have found your old friend again, you may keep it with you as you continue your psychic development.

SCRYING AND DIVINATION

Scrying is a form of divination. Its name comes from the word "descry"—to make out dimly. Scrying is usually done for the specific purpose of peering into the future. This may be done through a number of different tools. Reading a crystal ball, the smoke of a candle, or oil poured on water are all forms of visual scrying; however, any of the five senses may be used.

Scrying is actually a way of entering into a trance or altered state of consciousness. As you stare at an object and let your eyes go out of focus, a second image (a hologram) begins to appear. As you focus on the hologram, you step into a different time zone. Usually, scrying is used to see the future, but it is also possible to use scrying to visit the past. As long as you focus on the second image, you will stay in your psychic trance, and when you shift back to the reality of the moment, you will return to your normal state of consciousness.

Other forms of divination require that you manipulate a physical object and then enter your altered state of consciousness to interpret the patterns formed by your actions. Examples of this include the casting of runes or of coins used in I Ching, an ancient Chinese method of divination. Once these items are cast, the psychic uses the unconscious mind to make interpretations of the patterns they make, seeing what possibilities the future may hold in store.

CRYSTAL BALLS

When you think of a fortuneteller, chances are you imagine a woman in mystic clothing peering into a crystal ball in a dimly lit room. As she gazes into the sphere, she begins to see a glimpse of your future. She seems to go into some sort of a spell as she continues her monologue in her monotonous voice. You may wonder how it is that this magical crystal ball holds the information of your soul.

As you have learned in this book, every psychic you visit will read differently. Always be aware of the ones who are not true readers and use their skills for their own gain. Always compare what the psychic tells you with your own psychic knowledge of your guidance systems.

The truth is that the crystal ball is only a tool that helps induce an altered state of consciousness. The sphere becomes the window through which the psychic sees, hears, feels, tastes, or smells the vibrational level of the client's soul. Just as Edgar Cayce read the soul's history in the Akashic Records, the fortuneteller uses her altered state to access essentially the same information. All readers will gather different images through their own special techniques, which they have developed over time.

The crystal ball helps you go into your psychic trance. To try it, center on the ball, letting your eyes go out of focus, and ask your guidance system to provide you with the proper images related to the information that you are asking for from your Universal Mind. The more you practice and pay attention to your natural psychic intuition, the more you will be able to define the type of crystal ball that may be right for you.

Choosing the Right Crystal for You

Crystal balls come in various sizes and in a wide range of prices. Some can cost over $1,000 or even more, depending on the material they are made of. For some of you, the energy in rock crystals—those made of natural stone—corresponds with your psychic vibrational frequencies. In other words, the crystal may help open your psychic energy centers and make your intuitive connection stronger. If, on the other hand, your frequencies and those of the crystal ball are out of sync, it may interfere with your natural psychic ability.

A natural rock crystal is generally composed of a clear piece of quartz or beryl. It is believed that these substances contain magnetic properties that can help amplify your body's own energy field. The combination of the two energies is thought to help your connection to your soul and your ability to use your psychic gifts.

Different kinds of rock crystal have different vibration levels. The best way to find out which is right for you is to go to a store that sells several kinds of rock crystal balls so that you can compare how they resonate with your vibration level. If you are not affected by the energy in rock crystals, you may want to look at other types of crystal balls, such as those made of glass or Lucite.

Other Crystal Types

A crystal does not have to come in the shape of a ball or a sphere. It could be a natural shape or one that has been cut or faceted. You may find a crystal with the right vibration for you that you will want to keep with you all of the time. You might have it set into a piece of jewelry, to be used as a pendant, earrings, or a ring. You may find that when you wear, touch, or hold a special crystal, you are much more in tune with your psychic ability.

Your perfect crystal might not be a crystal at all. You might find a different type of stone that contains the right energy. You could even use a piece of metal, wood, or coral to help you get into your psychic trance zone. If you are sensitive to energy, the more you learn to work with it, the more in balance your psychic vibrations will be.

STONES AND RUNES

Some psychics use special stones that they cast in patterns to help produce psychic images. These stones could be from the ocean or the mountains. They may come from the same place or from many different locations. The more compatible the stones' energies are with your own, the more productive the readings will become.

You may want to begin collecting stones that have special meaning to you. Look for the right stones by placing your hands over them to see if you get a special feeling; you can also sit nearby and feel the energies emanating from them.

Feeling the energy of a stone or a group of stones may help induce a psychic trance. To try this, select some stones that have positive vibrations for you. You can hold them in your hands as you let your eyes go out of focus and enter your intuitive trance state. Now focus on the positive energy of the stones and ask that the right images be given to you to provide answers to your questions.

Once you've got a set of stones, you can begin developing a pattern in casting your stones. You could read them on the first throw or the second or the third. If you are not sure how many times you should cast the stones before reading their patterns, ask your unconscious mind for some guidance. When you have determined your course of action for casting, you can read your stones as often as you want. The more you do, the stronger your psychic images will begin to appear.

Casting Runes

Runes are ancient Norse symbols carved on small rocks or tiles. When a diviner casts runes, she can use the symbols to interpret the results in order to get answers to questions about the future. Make sure that the set of runes you select has an accompanying booklet that explains the meanings of the symbols and helps guide you on how to find the answers to your questions. Casting methods vary. You can select a single rune tile from a bag, cast them in lots, or place them in patterns as some people do with tarot cards.

I Ching

Another form of casting similar to rocks and runes is I Ching. To cast I Ching, you would use three coins. After throwing the coins six times, you get a hexagram. There are sixty-four possibilities, all of which are interpreted in the I Ching, or *Book of Changes*. I Ching doesn't exactly foretell the future—it is intended to guide the searcher to find his own answers.

OTHER TOOLS TO HELP YOU ENTER A TRANCE

There are other ways for psychics to enter trances that don't require purchasing a crystal or searching for stones; in fact, some items are as simple as a cup of tea. Psychics have long used the reading of tea leaves as a means of gazing into the future. If you would like to try reading tea leaves, brew yourself a pot using loose-leaf tea. Pour a cup, and let the tea leaves settle. As you drink the tea, communicate with your Belief. Consider your goals for the reading, and prepare to read the patterns in the leaves after you finish.

Here is a routine that you may want to try. After you finish your cup of tea, slowly turn the cup upside down and let any remaining liquid drain out into the saucer. Then, twirl the cup around three times, and turn it right side up again. Now, you can gaze into the tea leaves left in the bottom of the cup and intuitively read the patterns they formed.

Gazing into a bowl of dark liquid is one of the oldest forms of psychic foretelling. Early rituals included the use of blood and even the entrails of freshly sacrificed animals to help create an intuitive trance state.

If you try this, be sure to use a kind of tea that you enjoy and that is also relaxing. Let your eyes go out of focus, and let the information flow up to the surface of your conscious mind. If you find this method potentially helpful, you will want to develop your own ritual for focusing.

Coffee and Water

If you are a coffee drinker, you can use the movement of the cream as it mixes with the brown liquid to help you enter your trance state.

As you gaze into the cup, let your eyes go out of focus and become aware of your holographic psychic image as it emerges from the mixture. Once you have done this, you can contemplate the information you received as you sip your coffee. It is always a good idea to keep a notepad handy to help you remember your psychic information.

Nostradamus used a ritual of gazing into a bowl of water. Before he started his trance, he would dip a wand into the water and anoint himself. Then he would enter a trance that would let him see into the future.

If you want to abstain from coffee or tea, you can also use a bowl of water and add some oil to float on the surface. As the oil forms swirls, gaze into the bowl and let your eyes go out of focus. Drift into your psychic trance and collect the information that is given to you. When you are finished, take a deep breath, feel the peace and love of the Universal Mind, and slowly come back to the surface of your conscious mind.

Smoke, Steam, and Clouds

Smoke and steam can help induce psychic trances as well. Some psychics prefer to gaze into the steam and bubbles of boiling water. Native Americans use sweat lodges to help them create trance visions. The dimness of the light and the feeling of the heat help create altered states in the participants.

Gazing into fog, mist, and clouds are also excellent ways to produce psychic images. Another benefit to using these elements is that you have the opportunity to go to a special place where positive feelings and energy can amplify your intuitive images. Once you have had a positive experience at a special location that had clouds, mist, or fog, develop an anchor that will help put you there in your mind any time you want to connect to your psychic imagery. You can then use your special place as a tool and go there any time you want.

Mirror Images

A mirror is another tool that can help you enter into your psychic zone. You can certainly use a stationary mirror; another option is to find one that is rotated by a small motor. A black mirror is an excellent object to gaze into. To make one, find a picture frame that has a good piece of glass in it. Paint both the frame and the back side of the glass black. Assemble, and try using it as a psychic tool.

Have you ever looked out through a window that has old glass panes? The view is very wavy and a natural way to help your eyes go out of focus. Try getting comfortable and staring out through the window. As you enter a trance, let yourself become open to a hologram of psychic knowing.

Gaze into the mirror and let your mind go out of focus. Reflect on the images that you are intuitively experiencing. As you define your imagery and practice going out of focus, it will be easier for you to enter your intuitive trance state.

THE ART OF PALMISTRY

The ancient art of predicting the future by reading palms is thought to have originated in China or India as early as 3000 B.C.E. In Europe, witches and gypsies practiced it, and its popularity rose in the late nineteenth century as the public became more interested in spiritualism and the occult.

According to palmistry, the shape of your hands carries information about your physical and artistic traits. Lines, creases, and bumps found on the palms contain information about the past events of your life as well as the future; there is also information about your life map and soul's purpose. Some readers compare palmistry with astrology. They look for a relationship between the patterns in your palms and the signs of the zodiac.

If you are right-handed, your left hand indicates your life map while your right hand reveals how you have followed your soul's purpose. If you are left-handed, the roles of your hands are reversed.

The lines and markings in your palms may actually change over time to reflect the changes in your life. However, you can also actively work to change your palm patterns—thus changing the potential of your future—through the practice of Zen or yoga. Both of these practices, and yoga in particular, are spiritual belief systems that seek to liberate the spirit from physical matter for the purpose of becoming one with the Universal Mind.

CHAPTER 17

PSYCHIC HEALING

Faith healers have been a part of many cultures for millennia. It's possible that you could have a natural ability to be able to read someone's health condition. Or perhaps you could have psychic healing gifts that can help others. This chapter will discuss different types of psychic healing and help you figure out if this is one of your gifts. You will also learn about how a person's aura may be read and even manipulated for the purpose of better health.

PSYCHIC HEALING AND DIAGNOSIS

Witch doctors, shamans, and medicine men and women, among others, have long played important roles in the societies they lived in. Jesus Christ was hailed as a great healer. As late as the nineteenth century, magnetism and other methods of alternative healing enjoyed popularity, but many of the ancient healing arts eventually gave way to modern medicine. In fact, with the rise of wonder drugs, the popularity of the old ways of healing almost disappeared. Today, many people do not use their mind's ability for healing, but instead let their fate rest in the hands of doctors and drug companies. Perhaps there are still things to learn from the old forgotten ways.

Edgar Cayce and the Healing Arts Revival

It was Edgar Cayce who unwittingly became the focal point of the New Age movement, which swept the United States during the latter part of the twentieth century. Cayce's uncanny psychic ability to retrieve old healing remedies from the Akashic Records stored deep in the Universe changed the views of alternative medicine for many doubters.

For more information on Edgar Cayce, you can go to the ARE website at www.edgarcayce.org. ARE is the Association for Research and Enlightenment, located in Virginia Beach, Virginia. It was founded in 1931 and is still growing in membership today.

While in a deep, self-hypnotic trance, Cayce was able to scan a body with his mind and give a diagnosis based on what he saw. The subject did not even have to be in the same room for Cayce to give a reading and recommend treatment for the affliction. The language that Cayce used in a trance was not the lingo or jargon of modern medicine. The recommendations for treatments were given in terms that employed remedies long since forgotten. The diagnosis and treatments often focused on the body's energy system.

AURAS AND THE ANSWERS THEY HOLD

Your body is an energy grid. You have many energy centers, including your seven major chakras. When your energy is flowing evenly and all your centers are in balance, you are in tune mentally, physically, and spiritually with yourself and the Universe's energy. Your three minds are all working together in harmony with your Belief System and your guidance team. You are always connected to your third eye and completely centered and grounded with unconditionally loving and peaceful Universal Energy flowing over and around you.

Needless to say, to stay in this situation all the time is impossible. It is easy to be thrown off balance by life's resistances, both small and large. How soon you regain your balance and keep yourself in this positive energy can have a direct outcome on your own wellness. When positive energy flow is blocked, negative energy can manifest itself through a weakness in your body, which can result in illness.

The flow of energy, either positive or negative, through and around your body creates an energy field known as an aura. The more out of balance you are, the more your aura will reflect what is going on with you. That balance can be affected from moment to moment, and it is also influenced by the way you have taken care of yourself over a long period of time. The longer your aura remains unbalanced, the more susceptible you are to minor and major illnesses.

Reading an Aura

Each person will read auras a little differently. Your mental makeup will help indicate how you will best experience an aura reading. If you have a strong visual sense, you may be able to see an aura. If you have a strong hearing sense, you may hear—either by voice or by other sounds—the energy of an aura. If you are sensitive to touch, you may feel an aura. If you have a strong sense of smell, you may smell an aura, and if you have a strong sense of taste, you may actually taste it. Some people may be able to use all of their senses, while others rely on two or more that combine to provide them with the image. A feeling may create a picture, or a smell may produce a feeling.

Your first step is to identify how you read an aura. Once you've figured that out, the next step is to collect the information you receive. What does it mean? When you read someone's aura, can you use the information to develop a model of that person's health? If so, can you compare what you pick up to how this person actually feels?

Just about everyone has the ability to sense auras one way or another. If you are not aware of how you do it, you may not be paying attention to the clues you are giving yourself. Look for signals from your unconscious and your Universal Mind, and pay attention to your guidance systems.

Ask yourself what you can tell by the color of the aura, by sound, by feeling, by touch, by smell, or by taste. Can you feel negative or positive energy, and how can you apply what you feel to the actual health of the person? How about taste and smell? At first, you may want to keep a record of your observations to help validate the information you are receiving.

The next step is to apply your knowledge of how you read an aura to how you can develop an understanding of what you are reading. As you get experience, you will notice aura patterns that can give a sense of what the auras mean. These patterns will help you produce mental models of a positive, healthy aura and a negative, unhealthy one.

HEALING NEGATIVE ENERGIES

Once you have an understanding of positive and negative auras, you can begin to locate the specific areas of a person's body that emit negative energy. You may even be able to determine through your five senses the cause of the negative energy and develop a healing model for the negative aura. In other words, you may be able to diagnose what someone's negative aura means and then develop a model to change it.

Many people do not want to know anything that makes them feel responsible for someone else. They put up a defensive mental shield to block any such knowledge. If you have knowledge, don't expect others to accept what you know. All you can do is drop hints and hope they discover them.

There are two specific ways that healing energy works. It may come in through you, or you may let it flow out through you into the Universe. If you take in someone else's energy and are not grounded, you may be affected by what you are receiving. This sometimes happens to very kinesthetic people when they begin to study healing arts such as massage or Reiki. You may have taken in negative, unwanted energy naturally your whole life because of your psychic ability to feel the energy of others, both good and bad.

The other type of healer sends a strong Universal Energy through herself from an external source and into the client's body so that it flows through and over it, pushing out the negative energy. The sender often feels the power of the Universe, whereas the absorber is much more mellow. One potential problem for healers is to think they, and not the Universe, are responsible for the healing. If you are using your psychic healing ability, it is good to always remember where the true power comes from and to be grateful that by tapping into the flow, you are able to help others.

Develop a Model for Healing

What is going to be your strategy for healing? Can you develop a model in your mind of how you read someone's aura or energy? Which of the senses or combination of senses will you use—vision, hearing, feeling, taste, or smell? Can you use your psychic ability to change a negative aura into a positive one by playing with the images in your mind? Your psychic healing images are based on the way you understand the difference between negative and positive auras.

Are you a sender or a receiver? Your conscious mind may not know yet, but your unconscious and your Universal Mind do. You may feel the Universal Power in your fingers, or you may have the ability to snatch away someone's negative aura and send it out into the vast Universe to heal. If you are interested in further developing your psychic healing abilities, you may want to take classes in alternative healing, such as Reiki.

Whenever you work on yourself or someone else with healing energy, remember you are only doing something that is complementary to Western medicine. You are not offering a substitute for what a medical doctor would do.

You can always practice on yourself. Try slowly smoothing out your own aura, especially on days when you feel out of balance. Can you create an image of any negative energy that might be in you? If so, can you bring a positive image over the negative and feel yourself being filled with Universal peace and love from a healing energy at the same time? You may be amazed at the positive effect that healing energy can have on you or on someone else.

Exercise: Create Healing Energy

Now it's time to focus on bringing the Universal Force through you as a healing energy. Try this with yourself first. When you work with others, you will not be able to put yourself in the same state of relaxation as you can when you are working with yourself. However, you will still be able to develop a strong connection to the Universal Power.

* Take a deep breath and exhale slowly. Feel your body relaxing as you continue to breathe slowly in and out.

* When you are ready, focus on the Universe's peaceful, unconditional energy as it flows down through your crown chakra to your third eye. You may feel this healing force as it starts to flow down to your throat chakra. Let the healthy feeling of peace and love balance your throat center and continue on until all your energy centers are open and balanced with Universal, unconditional love and peace.

* You may thank the Universe that only the purest healing energy may flow through you to be passed on to the proper area of your or someone else's physical, mental, or spiritual body. You may be grateful that this Universal healing energy will allow the person for whom it is intended to find her balance and be tuned by it if she chooses to accept it.

* Now that you are centered, grounded, and protected by Universal Love, you may begin allowing the healing energy to flow to the areas that need healing. Remember, do it your way, the way that you have already identified with your strongest image senses. If you are clairvoyant, see. If you are clairaudient, hear. If you are clairsentient, feel. If you are strong in taste and smell imagery, use those senses to help amplify the Universal healing energy of peace and love that is flowing through you.

* If you are a receiver and are balanced and grounded, you may receive any negative energy so that it can be sent out into the Universe to be healed with peace and love.

The more you practice these concepts, adding the special things that work only for you, you will find yourself more and more in tune with the healing, peaceful, and loving energy of the Universe.

It is very important to remember that you are not the healer—the Universe is. Just remember to keep yourself grounded and in balance with the Universe's unconditional love so that you are the best conduit possible for the Universal healing energy.

Work with Someone Else

Once you are comfortable working with yourself, it is time to work with others. Use the knowledge that you have gained through your experiences, and work with someone you know who is receptive. Start slowly, and just read his or her aura so that you can develop a model of your subject's health. Look for positive and negative energy and physical, mental, and spiritual balance.

When you have decided on a healing strategy, start to bring positive energy in as you draw the negative energy out. This action is meant to help an individual connect to the Universal healing energy. Send the negative energy out to the Universe to be healed with peace and love.

REIKI AND OTHER HEALING MODALITIES

Healing may also be performed through a practice such as Reiki, massage, body scanning, or magnetic healing—some of the many alternative-healing methods available to you today.

The Art of Reiki

Reiki is an ancient healing practice that has undergone an impressive revival over the past few decades. After centuries of being forgotten, it was rediscovered in the early 1900s by Dr. Mikao Usui, a Japanese scholar and physician who stumbled upon it while researching sacred texts on the healing methods of Jesus. Usui worked diligently on developing the method of Reiki and using it to heal the poor, as well as teaching the technique to a few of his disciples.

Reiki attunes the energy centers in the body with the Universal Life Force. Its practitioners have specific hand positions that connect the energy with the client. They spend about five minutes in each position before moving to the next. At the same time, the practitioner may use his or her intuitive ability to help certain areas of the body to heal using the Life Force energy.

There are three degree levels in Reiki. Levels I and II are taught in a relatively short time span and can usually be completed within a weekend. Level III is the master level. Learning and practicing the beginning levels of Reiki is not very expensive, and it is a good way to begin experiencing alternative modalities. The fee for completing the third degree varies greatly from instructor to instructor and can run as high as $10,000.

Massage Therapy

Another healing technique is good old massage, because it uses hands-on techniques for comfort and healing. There are many different kinds of massage therapies, such as Swedish massage, which is very popular in health clubs and spas. Many massage therapists use their psychic ability to work the part of their client's body that has an energy block. A sensitive, in-tune, balanced massage therapist can also perform very effective healing practices by combining knowledge of the human body with intuitive abilities.

Body Scanning

Some of you may actually be able to scan a human body in your mind and develop an image of the person's health by using your five different senses. A medical intuitive can psychically read your body and come up with a diagnosis in actual medical terms. Each intuitive will work differently, but they all have a common goal: namely, the wellness of their clients. If you have the ability to scan a human body in your mind, you may want to get some training in the medical field so that you can effectively communicate the images you psychically receive.

Magnetic Healing

The principle of magnetic healing has been used since Franz Anton Mesmer worked with animal magnetism. He believed that he could rearrange invisible fluid in the body and bring about healing. Today there are magnets of different sizes that wearers believe can cure all kinds of ailments, such as arthritis, depression, and chronic pain. There are magnetic bracelets and magnets to put in your shoes, and many people claim to be helped by wearing them.

ARE YOU A MEDICAL INTUITIVE?

A medical intuitive is someone who has the ability to read others' health conditions and translate them into traditional medical terms. The diagnosis can then be treated medically. As with body scanning, you may want to seek the proper medical training to help you communicate what you already know psychically.

If you are already working in the medical field—whether as a doctor, nurse, or other medical professional—and you have the psychic gift of reading health conditions, then you are ready to develop your intuitive side. The first step is to understand what you sense psychically. This includes understanding your mental makeup and learning how your mind processes sensory information. The next step is to create a plan to help you further sharpen your natural psychic talents.

Do you know or think that you have a psychic gift to be a medical intuitive? If you have this ability, it does not mean that you have to announce it to everyone you know. Once you become aware of your potential, you are free to use it in your own best interests and those of others, in a way that is comfortable and positive for you. Here are some questions to help you identify your healing strengths:

* Do you have intuitive feelings about your or other people's health, or can you intuit other people's medical problems? If so, how?

* Do you see mental pictures, colors, or energy that show you a health problem?

* Do you hear voices or other sounds that indicate a medical problem?

* Do you get a feeling of health problems? If so, where do you feel it, mentally or physically?

* Can you touch and feel auras?

* Can you dowse a body for health problems?

* Do you experience smells that indicate health situations? It might be in the smell of someone's breath or body odor.

* Do you get a taste in your mouth that might give you a clue to a health condition?

You may even get combinations of sense images that can give you a clearer indication of your own or another person's health condition. If you have the psychic gift of knowing health conditions of others, you may want to develop it further.

If you want to develop your healing gifts, study as many alternative healing modalities as possible to help you decide which one works best for you and for those with whom you will work. The way you work with healing practices will be different from anyone else. The important thing is that whatever you do works best for yourself and others.

Your Responsibility As a Healer

Not everyone is comfortable with the role of healer. It is a special gift, and it comes with a lot of responsibilities. The first is to acknowledge that the real healer is a channel for the Universal Energy Force. The second is to understand that you are not a doctor or a nurse unless you are trained as one. You are only assisting a person to use her mental and spiritual selves in combination with the help of those trained in medicine to bring about wellness. As a psychic healer, you are not a substitute for a trained medical professional.

It is very important to take care of yourself mentally, physically, and spiritually so that you will be in tune to work with the healing energy of the Universe. The opportunity you've been given is unique and different from anyone else's on earth. It is your choice to be in tune with it.

So many gifted psychics, whether they are healers or work in other modalities, do not live up to the responsibility of keeping themselves in balance. The result is the work they do may not be their best, and they may not be able to use their intuitive healing gifts to the best of their potential.

SHARING YOUR PSYCHIC GIFTS

This book has allowed you to discover your incredible and unique psychic abilities. You have had an opportunity to try out many different psychic techniques. You have been shown how to identify and understand the intuitive gifts that you were born with. You have developed ways to be in tune with your internal and external guidance systems. You may have been able to meet and identify your guides, angels, or other spirits that are there to help guide and protect you. You have also learned about the importance of staying grounded through your connection to the unconditionally loving energy of the Universe, which is always there for you. Now it's time to incorporate these lessons into your daily life. This chapter will help you review what you have learned and give you some guidance to help you move psychically forward into the future.

WHAT IS THE NEXT STEP?

It is now time to consider what your next step is as you continue your psychic development. With your new knowledge and recently identified psychic skills, you have a wonderful opportunity to become in tune with your life purpose and your soul's journey. You are right on schedule to make a difference, not only in your life but very possibly in the lives of others as well.

You now know that you have an incredible team that is constantly there to help guide you in the future just as you were guided to read this book. All you need to do is to be open to the adventure that lies ahead of you.

Exercise: Find Your Direction

You can use your grounding technique to tune in to positive guidance from the Universe to help you find the direction your psychic gifts will take.

* Find your comfortable place, loosen your clothes, take a deep breath, exhale, and relax.

* You may close your eyes if you want or leave them open as you begin to feel the unconditionally loving energy of the Universe flow down from the top of your head to your third eye.

* Continue breathing in and out slowly while you begin to work your way down through your chakras, opening and balancing each one until you are completely immersed in this loving energy.

* When you are ready, slowly count yourself down from five to zero, focusing more and more on your connection to your Belief and your guides or angels.

* Use your anchors to help you focus on your positive psychic altered state as you strengthen your connection with the Universal Mind.

* When you arrive at zero, take some time to reflect on and enjoy the loving and peaceful energy of your Universal connection, knowing that your team is there to watch over and guide you.

Now thank your Belief for helping you determine the way your psychic gifts can be used to benefit humankind.

* You may ask your guides or angels or other spirits to communicate with you in a way that you will recognize and understand by signs that they give.

* Ask that you may use this information to help you become in tune with your soul's purpose.

* Give yourself a little time to be open for guidance.

* Suggest that after you count yourself back up to five that you will remain open to the messages and guidance from the Universe.

* To end your connection, take a comfortable breath and come back to full consciousness totally aware of your surroundings.

After you have practiced this technique a few times, you will be able to go directly to your altered state of consciousness without counting yourself down. All you need to do is to take a deep breath and change your focus to the unconditionally loving energy of the Universe, and you will be in your altered state. Remember that you should not go into a deep relaxed state when you are involved in an activity that requires your full attention, like driving.

Once you have counted yourself back to five and have come back to the surface of your mind, you can prepare yourself for guidance from your inner and outer team. As you have learned, that guidance may manifest itself in many different ways. It may come from inside yourself or from something you hear from someone else. You may hear it more than once.

PREPARE TO TAKE YOUR NEXT STEP

You can now call yourself a psychic and possibly even a medium. You have the unlimited power of the Universe ready and waiting to assist you. All you have to do is shift your focus, and you are in instant contact. With your ability comes the responsibility to use it for good.

> You have an inner guidance system that will let you know if you are going in a direction that is not in tune with your life journey. Pay attention to your warning system and take the time to get refocused on your life purpose.

So, what are you going to do with your new knowledge? You could use your psychic abilities for personal gain, but for how long? Remember what karma is. Are you willing to risk your investment in the future growth of your soul for momentary personal gain to satisfy your ego?

Many psychics have trouble reading for themselves. Don't be surprised if you do not receive the same insights for yourself as you do for others. You may find a trusted psychic friend who can share with you in like manner as you have the ability to share with him or her.

Prepare Physically

Part of your obligation is to keep yourself in tune physically for your psychic journey. If you are able, it is important that you find the time to stay as fit as possible. That means getting the right exercise and making the proper choice of healthful foods. The more you keep your physical body in condition to be a conduit for psychic energy, the better your connection to the Universal Mind will be. Your physical condition is a part of your psychic development.

Prepare Mentally

It is also important for you to keep yourself in as good a mental condition as possible for your upcoming psychic journey. Remember to keep a healthy mental perspective. Take the time to use your relaxation exercises to help keep your psychic energy in balance. Also use your mental anchors to trigger relaxed states during times when it is hard to escape the stresses that you encounter. The more time you can spend in a positive waking trance state, the more you will be mentally in tune with your psychic development.

Prepare Spiritually

The more grounded and comfortable you are with your personal Belief, the more in tune with your spirituality you will be. Make sure that you are in touch many times a day with your spirit guides, your angels, or whatever you believe is there to help guide you on your soul's journey. The more you are open to your internal and external guidance systems, the more you will learn to rely on the power and strength of the Universe's unconditionally loving energy. Remember always to be aware of keeping your chakra centers balanced and open to the peace and love of the Universe and to keep grounded in Universal golden light.

CONTINUE TO PRACTICE

Just as with any other talent, if you do not use your psychic talent, it will eventually dwindle away. Now that you have identified your psychic gifts, it is time for you to work with them on a steady basis. You may have more than one area that you want to develop. Make sure that you develop a plan that is workable for you. Many times people get very excited at learning something new at first, but if they do not quickly establish a routine, they can easily lose interest and abandon their project.

Set aside a period of time every day to work with your psychic ability. It doesn't have to be long, perhaps as little as fifteen minutes to start. The time you will need to take will depend on what you are working on and the potential need for companions in your work—whether you need to be alone, near people, or actually working with others. There may be times when you want to work alone in an altered state of focus with your guidance system. If you are reading people or energies, you will want to be in a place where you have access to different subjects.

Be aware that you may meet some resistance from other people, family, or friends. They may resent that you are spending time away from them. They may not believe in psychic abilities and may not be happy that you have that gift. They may not want you to mention the subject anywhere around them. You may have to find a way to balance your psychic development and your family and friends.

KEEP YOURSELF GROUNDED

One of the hazards that you may face as you become more and more in tune with your intuitive abilities is psychic energy buildup. What this means is that when you take a large amount of Universal Energy into your body, it is possible to build up a surplus. If it does not find an outlet, it will manifest itself in different ways, such as with an intense electrical tingling. As an example, if you are using your hands for healing and are bringing in the energy for that purpose, it is possible that you may feel prickly sensations in your hands.

It is always a good idea when you are working with energy to keep yourself grounded. There are several ways to do this. If the energy surplus is localized, such as in your hands or feet, the easy way is to touch the ground with the parts of your body that are overcharged. You can also shake your hands, your arms, or your fingers to help disperse the energy back into the Universe. Deep breathing is another excellent way as long as you let the energy flow out of your body when you exhale. If your entire body feels like it has been charged, you may want to exercise, go for a walk, or swim to help dissipate the energy.

Pay attention to how your psychic development is affecting you. When you remain focused on it for a period of time, are you able to clear it from your mind after you have finished a session? Are you able to sleep peacefully, or do you toss and turn?

Washing your hands and arms in cold water, bathing your feet, or immersing your whole self are all good ways to get rid of surplus energy. Remember that this charged energy is a healing energy and you can feel a sense of Universal peace and health as you let it flow back out into the Universe. To some people, drugs and alcohol may seem like a good way to disperse psychic energy, but they easily throw the body, mind, and spirit further out of balance and make it harder to stay grounded. The goal is to keep yourself in balance and in tune so that you retain the proper amount of healing and psychic energy.

THE UNIVERSAL OWNERSHIP OF YOUR POWER

Another problem many novice psychics face is learning to develop and use their psychic abilities while keeping in mind where the source of their power and knowledge originates. As you continue working on honing your psychic abilities, continually give thanks to the source of their origination, even if you are not completely sure what that source is. Ask yourself if these abilities are there for your responsible use and for the good of all or if you have the right to claim them as your own and use them for your personal short-term goals.

Owning something implies a certain amount of responsibility. If you impress on others that you have a psychic power, you will be expected to live up to your ability. Unfortunately your psychic power may not turn on and off like a light switch. Every time you receive psychic energy it may be a little different. Your connection to the Universe can sometimes be very strong and at other times very weak. Your job is to be ready to experience it when it is called for. The more you practice, the stronger your psychic connection will become.

If you take all the credit, then you will have to accept the failures that are bound to happen as you progress. If you acknowledge that the ownership is out in the Universe, then there are no failures, only honest attempts to succeed. Once you have established clear Universal ownership of your psychic abilities, not only in your mind but also in the minds of others, you will have the freedom to let your psychic gifts flow without the pressure to turn them on and perform.

When you relate your third "eye" to your excitement over your psychic development, you can keep a balance with your ego "I." Whenever you are aware that you are having a psychic insight, remember to focus on your third eye for a brief moment as you feel yourself surrounded by unconditional energy flowing down through your crown chakra, and give thanks and accept the psychic information that you receive from the Universe.

Develop a positive belief habit as you progress in your psychic growth. The more you give acknowledgment to your Belief and your guidance systems, the easier it will be to avoid the problems of the ego and the conflict of ownership. This will free you up to stay in proper focus.

ALWAYS BE A STUDENT

Always continue to be a student of the Universe. There is so much more that you can learn as you follow your soul's journey. Your teachers will appear when you are ready for the lesson. They may come at any time and from anywhere, while you are asleep, as an inner voice, or from someone you know or may have just met. Study, read, listen, and try out techniques to gain further knowledge.

Whenever you investigate new knowledge and skills that can enhance your abilities, it is good to always ask yourself how someone else's philosophies or techniques fit you. How do his or her ideas compare with how you believe?

What is right for someone else may not be right for your psychic development. Remember that you are the one who intuitively knows whether or not a piece of information fits into your life map.

THE WORLD IS WAITING

It is time for you to begin the incredible journey that lies ahead of you. You now have the knowledge and the tools to help you become in tune with your life purpose. You may want to refer to certain sections of this book until you feel confident and grounded in your Belief System. Remember that you may adapt any of the views stated here to fit how you intuitively feel. It is the purpose and significance of your journey that is important. Don't attempt to take an approach that does not feel right for you.

It is hoped that you now know that you have a life purpose and that your psychic ability is a major part of it. If you accept the opportunity that you are offered, you may never view the world in the same way again. It may become rich in meaning and mystery and full of constant discovery.

Your friends, family, and coworkers may see something in you that they did not notice before. You may find that complete strangers are drawn to have a conversation with you. Every day you may notice miracles that have always existed around you but that you failed to see before. Life has the potential of taking on a completely new and exciting adventure for you. There is no way that you can successfully explain the incredible feeling of being in tune with your life map.

This book has a piece of your life map, waiting for you to use it on your soul's journey. Your guides, angels, or spirits and the Universe have sent it to you. Every reader has been sent one. Have you discovered yours yet? Only you can recognize it. It is something that can help you rediscover and develop the psychic abilities that are a part of your soul's rich heritage. If you haven't discovered it yet, don't worry. It will be revealed to you when it is time for you to understand it if you so choose. Just be aware, go forward, and believe in your psychic gifts.

APPENDIX

GLOSSARY OF TERMS

Akashic Book of Records
A book that contains detailed records of every soul's existence.

altered state of consciousness
A trance-like condition in which the conscious mind does not make critical decisions but accepts the images it receives through the five senses.

anchor
A physical or nonphysical reminder that re-creates a previous emotional state.

angel
A positive entity whose purpose is to help you. In Christianity, a messenger of God.

astral plane
A place outside of your physical body that can be visited via astral projection. An astral plane is not of the earth's plane.

astral projection
When a person leaves the physical body and travels to other places in or out of the earth's plane.

astrology
A system of predicting future events through studying the movement of celestial bodies.

aura
The energy field around a person or object.

automatic writing
Writing that comes from your unconscious mind while in a light trance state.

Belief System
A set of standards by which one lives one's life, usually connected to a higher power.

body scanning
The ability to look psychically into and around a human body for the purpose of determining the subject's health. Body scanning can be experienced through any of the five different senses.

chakras
The body's energy centers.

channel
A conduit. A psychic channel is a person through which another spirit or entity can communicate.

clairaudience
The gathering of psychic information through the hearing sense.

clairsentience
The gathering of psychic information through the sense of feeling.

clairvoyance

The gathering of psychic information psychically through the senses.

comfort zone

A place or state of mind where you feel safe and have little or no anxiety.

conscious mind

The surface of the mind; the communication center where you process thoughts and ideas.

daimons

Divine spirits that offer wisdom, usually through internal voices.

deductive psychic image

A psychic image that comes from your unconscious mind's ability to take in external sensory stimuli.

déjà vu

The feeling that you have been someplace or done something before.

divination

The ability to predict the future or find objects by information gathered through psychic abilities. Many different tools can be used to aid in divination. See "scrying."

EMF meter
An instrument that measures electromagnetic fields and is often used for ghost hunting.

exorcism
A rite to get rid of evil spirits, usually performed by a priest.

fairy
A form of spirit resembling a small person; fairies are said to have magical powers.

free will
The freedom to choose—to follow or reject the soul's purpose.

gatekeeper
A spirit guide that helps control your connection with the spirit world; gatekeepers are a source of protection from unwanted contact from the Other Side.

goal-focused psychic intuition
A combination of deductive and random intuition used in an effort to gain specific insights.

guidance system
The guidance system has two parts: internal and external. Your internal guidance system is the connection to and advice from whatever it is you believe in—God, angels, guides, or other beings. Your external guidance system is made up of the elements that go with you to help you on your soul's journey.

guide
A spirit energy whose purpose is to watch over the person to whom it is connected.

hologram
A three-dimensional image.

hypnosis
An altered state of consciousness in which the unconscious mind accepts suggestions.

I Ching
An ancient Chinese method of divination consisting of sixty-four hexagrams, each with a different meaning.

intuition
The ability to know things that are not related to conscious reasoning.

karma
Unresolved situations from past lives that carry over into the current life.

kinesthetic
Related to the sense of touch or feeling.

life map
Potential conditions for soul development that each person is born with; people's free will to make life choices determines whether they will meet their potential.

life work
The plan for your soul's development during your present lifetime, also referred to as your life map.

lucid dream
A dream that starts in your dream state and continues into your waking state.

magnetism
Power that can bring about healing without using traditional medicine.

medical intuitive
A person with the psychic gift of knowing the health condition of others.

medium
A person through whom the deceased can communicate with the living.

mental telepathy
Nonverbal communication through the mind.

miracle
An occurrence with no explanation based on reality, usually attributed to a supernatural power that intervenes in the normal course of events.

near-death experience
A form of out-of-body experience.

neurolinguistic programming (NLP)
The process of changing or reframing how the unconscious mind holds a belief; the reframe process happens when the unconscious mind accepts a mental image that is different from one already in place.

out-of-body experience
When your mental body leaves your physical body and goes someplace else.

palmistry
The ability to read the future by studying the lines and shapes of the palm of the hand.

postcognition
A visual psychic image that shows how an event from the past actually happened; also known as retrocognition.

power animal
A spirit animal that acts as a guide.

precognition
The knowledge of something that may happen in the future.

premonition
The feeling that something is going to happen before it does.

psychic
Relating to sources of knowledge that have no scientifically proven basis, such as intuition or the supernatural.

random psychic intuition
A psychic experience that comes at a time when it is unexpected and sometimes unwanted.

reading
Receiving information that psychically relates to a person, place, or object.

reframe
The installation of a new habit into the unconscious mind.

Reiki
A practice of transferring healing energy from the Universal Life Force through the practitioner to the subject.

remote viewing
A form of astral projection in which the subject is able to psychically view a specific location and to report what he or she observes.

retrocognition
Psychic information gathered from the past; also known as post-cognition.

rune
A letter of the ancient alphabet used by Germanic peoples from approximately the third to thirteenth centuries.

Sanskrit
The ancient language of the Hindu people of India.

script
The words used to help induce, deepen, and bring about a specific goal in a state of hypnosis.

scrying
Using visual aids to help produce the proper trance to see into the future.

second sight
A term often used to describe a person who has the gift of psychically gathering information. See "clairvoyance."

shaman
A tribal medicine man or woman, priest, or sorcerer.

spirit
A nonphysical entity.

Spiritualism
A Christian religion that includes the belief that spirits can communicate with the living through a medium.

subconscious
See "unconscious mind."

table tipping
The movement of a table by a spirit communicating through a system of raps or taps produced when the leg of the tipped table strikes the floor.

telepathy
Communication of one mind with another by some means beyond normal sensory perception.

third eye
The center of the forehead, which may feel tight and swollen by strong emotions and through which many believe the Universal Mind is contacted.

time-bending
Merging different time periods for the purpose of healing the past.

trance
An altered state of consciousness in which the unconscious mind is open to suggestion and loses its ability to make critical decisions.

trance channeler
A person in a deep trance who, without conscious awareness, becomes the means through which a spirit can communicate.

unconscious mind

The storage area of the mind that contains all your past experiences; also referred to as the subconscious.

Universal Energy

A form of energy that comes from your Belief System.

Universal Flow

The energy that is transmitted to and through you by the Universe or your Belief System.

Universal Mind

The part of your soul where you enlist the unknown to give you strength and produce miracles.

INDEX